DAY SKIPPER
EXERCISES FOR
SAIL & POWER

Other titles by the same authors

Day Skipper for Sail & Power
3rd edition
ISBN 9781472944818

Day Skipper for Sail & Power is a major reference book for anyone following the RYA Day Skipper course. Brought thoroughly up to date with new developments and covering all the theory and practical aspects of the RYA Day Skipper Certificate with full colour photography, helpful diagrams and worked examples, it is also a clear and comprehensive manual for anyone intending to make coastal passages in a small boat.

Yachtmaster for Sail & Power
5th edition
ISBN 9781472973511

A major reference book that has proved invaluable for the many sailors following the RHA Coastal Skipper/Yachtmaster Offshore course. This highly respected and refreshingly practical study guide covers the whole syllabus in detail, all illustrated with cover photographs, charts and worked examples throughout.

Yachtmaster Exercises for Sail & Power
4th edition
ISBN 9781472949400

This companion volume to *Yachtmaster for Sail & Power* provides further navigational practice for anyone studying the RYA Yachtmaster syllabus. It is packed with practice questions and test papers, and comes with a free practice chart which, together with extracts from tide tables, almanacs and pilotage notes, enables students to work on real sailing scenarios and plot their own courses without the need for any other material. This new edition has been revised throughout with new practice questions and examples as well as new photography and diagrams.

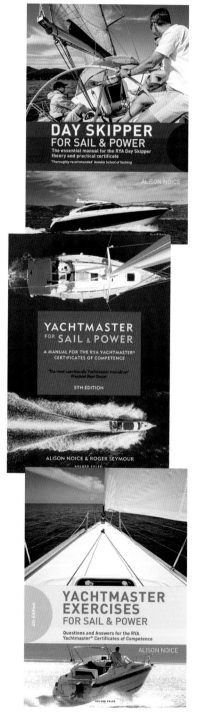

DAY SKIPPER
EXERCISES FOR
SAIL & POWER

2nd edition

ALISON NOICE &
ROGER SEYMOUR

ADLARD
COLES

LONDON · OXFORD · NEW YORK · NEW DELHI · SYDNEY

ADLARD COLES
Bloomsbury Publishing Plc
50 Bedford Square, London, WC1B 3DP, UK

BLOOMSBURY, ADLARD COLES and the Adlard Coles logo are
trademarks of Bloomsbury Publishing Plc

First published in Great Britain 2008
This edition published 2020

A catalogue record for this book is available from the British Library

Library of Congress Cataloguing-in-Publication data has been applied for

ISBN: 9781472973764

10 9 8 7 6 5 4 3 2 1

Typeset in Kievit 11/13pt by Margaret Brain
Printed and bound in India by Replika Press Pvt. Ltd.

To find out more about our authors and books visit www.bloomsbury.com
and sign up for our newsletters

Contents

Exercises **1**

Test Papers **37**

Answers (sections 1 to 15 and Test Papers 16 to 19) **47–101**

Extracts **102**

Acknowledgements

Thank you to all the people who have helped with the production of these exercises and to the companies who willingly gave permission to use their photographs and other material:

Adlard Coles Nautical
Alamy
Bruce Anchors
Cranchi Boats
Hamble School of Yachting
Getty Images
Imray Laurie, Norie & Wilson Ltd
Ken Waylen
McMurdo
Ofcom
Pains Wessex Safety Systems

Raymarine
Reeds Nautical Almanac
Royal Yachting Association
Simrad Yachting
Stanford Maritime
Trinity House
UK Hydrographic Office
Volvo Penta UK
www.stevenrichard.com
Yaesu

Special thanks to Peter Noice for the majority of the photographs in this book, and much assistance in its writing.

Preface to the 2nd edition

This book was originally conceived by Alison and I too now have had the honour of contributing, in however minor a way. I have updated the contents to compliment her writing, and in this way, I can continue to work in spirit with a great friend.

This book has consistently remained useful as a training or reference work to both beginners and experts alike over many seasons. I have intentionally retained the style and humour, focusing on covering integration of modern technology with more traditional methods, where possible and in a practical manner.

I have revisited the text to ensure it is timely and relevant in the contemporary world for all those wishing to safely enjoy their adventures on the water.

Roger Seymour

Introduction

When writing these exercises I assumed that the reader had little or no previous nautical knowledge before tackling their first Royal Yachting Association navigation course or began by reading a book such as *Day Skipper for Sail & Power*.

This book covers all the subjects in the RYA Day Skipper theory syllabus together with some practical subjects, such as VHF radio and engine maintenance. Each exercise is carefully graded so that you get sufficient practice on core subjects before progressing to the more complex ones. I have placed emphasis on the use of modern electronic equipment without neglecting the vital traditional skills that need to be used in conjunction with the former.

A comprehensive step-by-step answer section shows how the solution was found and the layout should help to establish an order of working when solving tidal height and course to steer problems. A Stanfords Channel Islands chart has been included so that you can practise your new skills in the comfort of your own home – all the equipment you need is a large pair of dividers, a Portland-type navigational plotter, a couple of soft 2B pencils and a good plastic eraser.

Remember that all this knowledge is no substitute for the real thing. A few days spent skippering or crewing a boat on a coastal cruise is of more value than months spent in a classroom.

Good luck, keep safe but above all, *have fun*.

Alison Noice

EXERCISES

1 Seamanship and Ropework

1.1a

Which letters in Figure 1.1a refer to the following parts of a sailing yacht?

1) Companionway

2) Stern

3) Grab rail

4) Bow roller

5) Boom

6) Main sheet

7) Tiller

8) Forestay

9) Cockpit

10) Stanchion

11) Fender

12) Keel

13) Rudder

14) Foresail sheet

15) Fairlead

16) Forehatch

17) Backstay

18) Shroud

19) Lifebuoy

20) Winch

Fig 1.1a *Parts of a sailing yacht.*

EXERCISES

1.1b

Which letters in Figure 1.1b refer to the following parts of the motor cruiser?

1) Saloon doors
2) Anchor line
3) Transom
4) Tender
5) Chine
6) Masthead light
7) Fly bridge
8) Pulpit
9) Bathing platform
10) Fairlead
11) Rubbing strake
12) Davit
13) Engine air intake
14) Foredeck
15) Radio antenna
16) Radar antenna
17) Cockpit

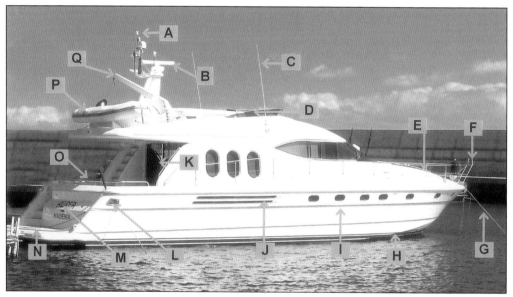

Fig. 1.1b *Parts of a motor cruiser.*

1.2

Three types of powered craft are shown in Figure 1.2. Which letter refers to the following?

1) Semi displacement
2) Fly bridge cruiser
3) Displacement

Fig 1.2 *Types of powered craft.*

EXERCISES

1.3

Three different types of keel configuration are shown in Figure 1.3. Which letter refers to the following?

1) Long keel   2) Bilge keel   3) Fin and skeg

Fig 1.3 *Types of keel.*

1.4

Three knots or bends are shown in Figure 1.4.

What is the name of each knot?

What would you use it for?

Give reasons.

Fig 1.4 *Knots and bends.*

1.5

Name the different lines in Figure 1.5, which are used to secure the boats alongside.

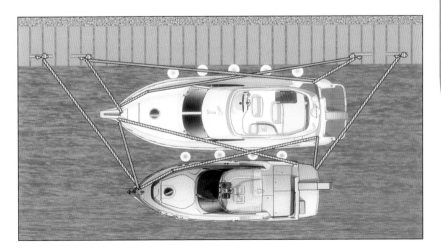

Fig 1.5 *Lines.*

3

1.6
Name the types of anchor shown in Figure 1.6.

Fig 1.6 *Anchors.*

1.7
Many factors need to be considered when selecting a good, safe anchorage for the night. Suggest five.

1.8
You are intending to purchase some anchor line. What type of rope should you buy?

1.9
What is the minimum length of cable that should be used in fair conditions when anchoring in a maximum depth of 7m of water:

a) using all chain?

b) using a combination of chain and warp?

1.10

a) What is the national maritime ensign of the United Kingdom?

b) What is the name of the small triangular flag flown by some craft?

c) What flag should be flown on the starboard side of the mast when visiting another country?

2 Introduction to Chartwork

Use the Stanfords Channel Islands chart to answer to questions 2.7 to 2.10.

2.1
The Stanfords Channel Islands chart is based on the European Datum 1950. Explain why we might need to know this when using a GNSS (Global Navigation Satellite System) receiver?

2.2
What is the significance of the pale orange areas on the chart?

2.3
What is the meaning of the following chart symbols?

Fig 2.1 *Chart symbols.*

2.4
Complete the following sentence:

The paler blue shading shows depths of less than................metres.

2.5
The chart is Mercator projection.

Why is it important to know this information?

2.6
Pair the directions and bearings from the two lists below:

a)	SW	i)	000°
b)	E	ii)	225°
c)	NW	iii)	135°
d)	W	iv)	180°
e)	N	v)	270°
f)	SE	vi)	315°
g)	NE	vii)	090°
h)	S	viii)	045°

2.7

What is the latitude and longitude of the following features?

a) Point Corbière Lighthouse on the SW corner of Jersey?

b) The spire on Mont Saint-Michel (bottom right-hand corner of the chart)?

c) The drying wreck on the Plateau des Minquiers?

2.8

Identify the features at the following positions:

a) 011°T from Grand Léjon Lighthouse 6.7 miles

b) 48° 45'.3N 002° 44'.0W

c) 48° 34'.4N 002° 41'.0W

2.9

Why is anchoring not allowed in the area off Surville (approx. 49° 17'N 01° 43'W)?

2.10

Where is information about chart corrections published?

Getting to grips with the chart.

3 Buoys, Beacons and Lights

Use the Stanfords Channel Islands chart to answer questions 3.1, 3.3, 3.4 and 3.5.

3.1
What is the significance of the buoys in the following positions?

a) 48° 53'.2N 002° 51'.8W

b) 48° 52'.2N 001° 46'.4W

c) 48° 39'.4N 002° 03'.6W. See inset at the bottom of the chart.

3.2
What is the colour and sequence of the light on the following buoys and beacons?

Fig 3.1 *Lights on buoys.*

3.3
a) Describe the light characteristics of the light on St Martin's Point (SE Guernsey).

b) What is the height of the light above Mean High Water Springs (MHWS)?

c) What is the nominal range of the light?

d) How often does the horn sound in fog?

3.4
You are on a position line 200°T from Grand Léjon lighthouse (48° 45'.0N 002° 40'.0W).

Are you in the red or the white sector of the light?

3.5
Is it possible to see Grosnez Point light (on the north-west corner of Jersey) from the anchorage in Saint Ouen's Bay?

3.6

a) Is the buoy in Figure 3.2 used as a permanent or a temporary mark?

b) Is the colour of the light:

    1) yellow?   2) blue?   3) yellow and blue?

3.7

Explain the difference between an isophase light, a flashing light and an occulting light.

Fig 3.2 *Wreck buoy.*

3.8

You are heading in an easterly direction as you enter a buoyed harbour.

Will you alter course to port, to starboard or either way when you see buoys with the following top marks immediately ahead (Fig 3.3)?

    a)   b)   c)   d)   e)

Fig 3.3 *Top marks.*

3.9

In Figure 3.4, the preferred channel is on the left of the picture. Would you expect to see beacon A or beacon B placed at the junction of the two channels?

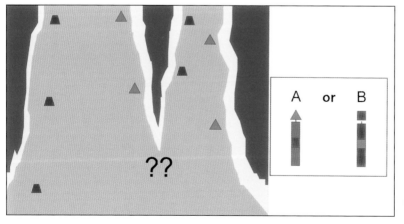

A or B

??

Fig 3.4 *Channel markers.*

3.10

You are entering a river in an area that uses the IALA 'B' buoyage system. What is the shape and colour of the buoy that you leave to starboard?

4 Compass and Position Fixing

Use the Stanfords Channel Islands chart for this exercise. Plot the fixes in questions 4.7 to 4.10 using the NE corner of the chart. Use 3°W variation.

4.1
Look at the compass rose just north-east of St Malo on the Stanfords Channel Islands chart. What is the magnetic variation in 2008?

4.2
What will be the MAGNETIC course for the following?

a) 235°T Variation 3°W

b) 356°T Variation 7°W

c) 135°T Variation 9°E

d) 002°T Variation 11°E

4.3
What will be the TRUE course for the following?

a) 285°M Variation 3°W

b) 004°M Variation 5°W

c) 207°M Variation 6°E

d) 357°M Variation 5°E

Fig 4.1 *A modern steering compass.*

4.4
The compass is affected by an error called deviation. What are some of the possible causes?

4.5
A boat is entering the port of St Malo using the Chenal de la Petite Porte leading line. The tide is slack so the skipper decides to do a compass check. With the leading lights in line the compass reads 135°C. The variation is 3°W.

What is the deviation on this heading?

4.6
A boat is entering St Helier (south coast of Jersey) in a slack tidal stream using the leading line from the south. With the leading lights in line, the compass reads 020°C. The variation is 3°W.

What is the deviation on this heading?

4.7

The navigator of a boat on passage along the northern side of the Contentin Peninsula records the following information in the ship's log book at 0530 just as dawn breaks:

La Noire Pierre WCM (west cardinal mark)   077°M

Sectored light south of Cap Levi   143°M

Log reads 29.6. Depth sounder reads 42 metres

Plot the 0530 fix and give the latitude and longitude.

4.8

Plot the boat's position at 0600 from the following log entry and give the latitude and longitude:

Ile Pelée Oc(2)WR light   149°M

Fl(3)WR Lt on Cherbourg breakwater   223°M

Water tower   186°M

Log reads 32.7

4.9

At 0640 the following bearings are plotted by the (very busy) navigator.

Raz de Bannes beacon   213°M

CH1 Safe water mark   050°M

Log reads 37.1

Comment on the reliability of this fix.

4.10

The navigator has entered a waypoint into the GNSS that is 0.5M due north of Basse Bréfort buoy. At 0700, the log reads 38.6 and the bearing and distance to the waypoint is shown as: 279°T distance 1.8M.

Plot the 0700 fix and give the latitude and longitude.

5 Tidal Streams

Use the tidal diamond table at the foot of the Stanfords Channel Islands chart and the tidal stream atlas (Extracts 2A and 2B). Time zone for answers = BST.

5.1

Looking at the tidal diamond table on the Channel Islands chart, what is the direction and rate of the tidal stream in the Big Russel (east of Guernsey) at:

a) HW St Helier at neaps?

b) 4hrs before HW St Helier at springs?

c) 3hrs before HW St Helier, midway between springs and neaps?

5.2

HW St Helier is at 0830 and it is springs. Tidal diamond Ⓐ shows the direction and rate of the tidal stream as 090°T 3.4kn. Between which times could you assume that the rate is as stated?

5.3

HW St Helier is at 1400. Your passage between ports will take approximately 30mins and you intend to leave at 1730. Which tidal hour will you use?

The fast stream off Guernsey causes swirling water around Roustel Beacon.

5.4

Using the same tidal diamond table on the chart and the tide table for St Helier (Extract 3), what is the direction and rate of the tidal stream 3M south of the Island of Jersey on:

a) Wednesday 16 May, between 0612 and 0712 BST?

b) Sunday 24 June, between 1550 and 1650 BST?

c) Sunday 5 August, between 0807 and 0907 BST?

5.5

To which standard port do you refer when using the tidal stream atlas (Extracts 2A and 2B)?

5.6

Using the tidal stream atlas and a plotter to measure direction:

a) What is the direction and rate of the tidal stream along the north-west coast of Jersey 5hrs after HW Dover at neaps?

b) What is the direction and rate of the stream to the east of the island of Alderney 1hr after HW Dover at springs?

c) What is the direction and rate of the stream south of the French port of Carteret 2hrs before HW Dover when the tide is at mid range?

5.7

Using the tidal stream atlas at the back of the book and the plotter, calculate the direction and rate of the tidal stream (all times are in BST):

a) North-west of Cherbourg on Thursday 17 May between 1335 and 1435?

b) Close to the south-west corner of Guernsey on Sunday 24 June between 1443 and 1543?

c) Close to the west of Plateau de Barnouic on Saturday 28 July between 2140 and 2240?

5.8

It is Saturday 26 May. Between which times (BST) during the afternoon will the stream be running at its strongest between Alderney and France?

5.9

A skipper wishes to take a favourable tide from an anchorage off Port de Diélette to Sark. At what time on the morning of Tuesday 10 July does the stream turn in his favour?

5.10

Between which times, during the afternoon of Wednesday 15 August, will the tidal stream be slack to the south of Jersey?

The strong tidal stream at the Columbia River entrance.

6 Dead Reckoning and Estimated Position

Use Stanfords Channel Islands chart and 3°W variation. All times are in BST.

6.1

Use the following log book extract to plot the dead reckoning position of a boat en route from Port de Diélette to Jersey.

Time	Log	Co (°M)	Wind	L'way	Notes
0800	0.0	195°	E3	Nil	At Q(9)15s off Cap de Flamanville
0820	2.0	195°	E3	Nil	Altered course 185°M
0900	6.2	185°	E3	Nil	Off Basse Bihard. Altered course 190°M
0940	10.4	190°	E1	Nil	Trois Grunes. DR position plotted

Fig 6.1 *Log entry for question 6.1.*

6.2

At 1500, a boat is in position 49° 20'.9N 002° 14'.0W. The heading is 098°M and the boat speed is 6kn. The tidal stream from 1500 to 1600 has been calculated as 070°T, 1.6kn.

a) Plot the estimated position at 1600.

b) What is the course over the ground?

c) What is the speed over the ground?

6.3

At 1230 a boat is in position 127°T, 4.1M from the Q(3)10s buoy to the east of Sark. It is heading 005°M and the boat speed is 7.7kn. The tidal stream from 1230–1330 is calculated as 194°T, 2.4kn.

a) Plot the estimated position at 1330 and give the latitude and longitude.

b) What is the speed over the ground?

6.4

The skipper of a motor cruiser has used a GNSS waypoint at the centre of the compass rose (south of Alderney) to assist with position fixing. At 1430, the GNSS gives the bearing and distance to this waypoint as 030°T, 3.2M.

a) Plot the 1430 position.

b) The helmsman is steering a course of 150°M at 16 knots. HW St Helier is at 2000 and it is a spring tide. Use tidal diamond Ⓖ to plot the estimated position at 1500.

c) Give the 1500 position in latitude and longitude.

6.5

At 1653 on Wednesday 6 June, a yacht on passage from Sark to Jersey is in position 49° 21'.7N 002° 21'.7W. The log reads 10.1 and the course is 160°M. At 1753, when the log reads 15.6, the skipper works up an EP on the chart using the tidal stream atlas.

a) How far has the yacht travelled through the water between 1653 and 1753?

b) What is the time of HW Dover? Is it neaps, springs or mid range?

c) Use the tidal stream atlas at the end of the book to calculate the direction and rate of the tidal stream from 1653–1753.

d) Plot the estimated position and give the latitude and longitude at 1753.

e) What is speed over the ground (SOG) and the course over the ground (COG)?

6.6

At 0822 on Wednesday 4 July, a yacht is positioned on the 13.7m charted depth at the south-western end of Rigdon Bank (NW Jersey). The visibility is good and the helmsman is steering an average course of 034°M at 5kn while on passage to Diélette from Jersey.

a) Use tidal diamond ◇J to plot the EP for 0922.

b) Will the yacht be clear of the Paternosters or will it have to tack?

c) If it has to tack, what landmark could the navigator use to check that he tacks before the rocks are reached?

6.7

Use the following log book extract to plot the EP of a trawler working south of Guernsey on Wednesday 29 August.

Time	Log	Co (°M)	Wind	L'way	Depth	Notes
0857	3.4	140°	SW3	Nil	45m	0.5 mile 180°T from St Martin's Point
0927	9.2	140°	SW3	Nil	51m	Altered course 212°M
0945	12.8	212°	SW4	Nil	49m	Altered course 175°M
1027	18.0	175°	SW4	Nil	40m	EP using ◇J

Fig 6.2 *Log entry for question 6.7.*

7 Course to Steer

Use Stanfords Channel Islands chart and 3°W variation. All times are in BST.

Questions 1–4 are to be plotted on the bottom left corner of the chart.

Questions 5–7 are south and east of Alderney.

7.1

At 0800 a yacht is close to Caffa East Cardinal beacon (bottom left-hand corner of chart).

a) What is the magnetic course to steer to a waypoint positioned 1 mile due west of Petit Léjon beacon? The boat speed is 5kn. The tidal stream is 070°T, 2.1kn.

b) What is the speed over the ground?

7.2

At 0900 a diving boat is positioned over the wreck at 48° 45'.0N 002° 44'.8W.

a) What is the magnetic course to steer to the 11m charted depth close to Madeux beacon (near St Quay-Portrieux)? The boat speed is 6.0kn. The tidal stream is 325°T, 1.5kn.

b) What is the speed over the ground?

c) At the beginning of the passage will Madeux beacon be seen:

i) To port?　　ii) To starboard?　　iii) Ahead?

Motor cruiser on passage.

7.3

At 1000 a motor cruiser is in position 48° 48'.8N 002° 48'.5W.

a) What is the magnetic course to steer to a waypoint positioned 1 mile due north of Les Justières beacon (just north of Erquy)? The boat speed is 28kn. The tidal stream is 100°T, 3.0kn.

b) What is the speed over the ground?

c) Approximately how long will the passage take?

7.4

At 1100 a yacht is in position 063°T, 1.6M from Binic Oc(3)12s light (48° 36'.2N 002° 49'.0W).

a) What is the magnetic course to steer to the marked anchorage at Erquy?
Boat speed = 5.5kn.
The tidal stream from 1100–1200 = 125°T 1.0kn.
    1200–1300 = 156°T 0.7kn.

b) Will the yacht remain on the drawn track for the whole time?

c) How could the skipper use the GNSS to check how close to the track he is?

7.5

At 0908 on Thursday 23 August, a yacht is in position 49° 45'.0N 002° 00'.0W.

a) What is the magnetic course to steer to a waypoint at 49° 37'.7N 002° 03'.3W? Use tidal diamond Ⓑ and a boat speed of 6kn.

b) What is the SOG?

7.6

At 1420 on Friday 18 May a motor cruiser is positioned at the southern tip of Banc de la Schôle (about 12M NE of Guernsey).

a) What is the magnetic course to steer to a position on the leading line 040°T, 6.8M from the Al WR 10s light at St Peter Port. Use the tidal stream atlas pages at the back of the book. Boat speed is 15kn.

b) What is the course to steer if there is a fresh northerly wind giving 10° leeway?

7.7

A navigator has entered a waypoint at the centre of the compass rose just south of the Alderney race. He will use the waypoint to help him fix position easily when using the GNSS. The GNSS shows that the bearing and distance to this waypoint is 100°T 6.8M at 1124 BST on Tuesday 5 June. The boat speed is 5kn. Use tidal diamond Ⓒ for the first hour then diamond Ⓑ.

a) What is the magnetic course to steer to a further waypoint at 49° 43'.9N 002° 04'.0W?

b) Will the yacht be clear of the overfalls on Race Rock?

8 Tidal Heights

Refer to the Almanac extracts at the end of the book where necessary. All times are given in BST; please give answers in BST.

8.1

Which letters in Figure 8.1 refer to the following?

i) Mean High Water Springs

ii) Highest Astronomical Tide

iii) Charted depth

iv) Drying height

v) Mean Low Water Springs

vi) Height of tide

vii) Vertical clearance

viii) Depth of water

ix) Mean High Water Neaps

x) Charted height

xi) Mean Low Water Neaps

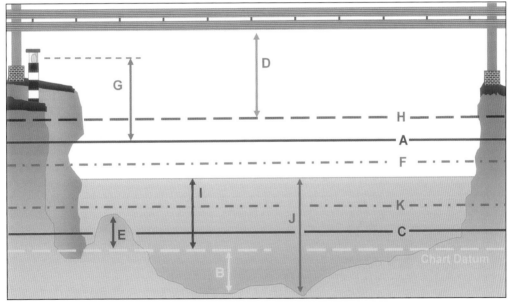

Fig 8.1 *Tidal heights.*

8.2

If the height of tide is 3.0m:

a) What is the depth of water in position 48° 59'.1N 001° 39'.2W?

b) What is the depth of water 019°T, 2.1M from the breakwater light at Diélette? (West side of the Contentin Peninsula – just north of Cap de Flamanville).

EXERCISES

8.3

Use the tidal levels information for St Helier in Figure 8.2 to calculate:

a) The depth of water at the marked anchorage in St Aubin Bay (Jersey, south coast) at MHWS.

b) The depth of water on the Écrevière Bank (Les Écrehou, NE of Jersey) at MLWN.

Standard Port ST HELIER			
Height (metres)			
MHWS	MHWN	MLWN	MLWS
11.0	8.1	4.0	1.4

Fig 8.2 *Tidal heights.*

8.4

What are the times and heights of HW:

a) At breakfast time on Tuesday 26 June at Dover?

b) During the evening of Thursday 2 August at St Helier?

c) During the early afternoon of Saturday 7 July at Cherbourg?

8.5

Use the tide table for St Helier to calculate the range of the tide:

a) During the late evening and early morning of 30 and 31 August? Is it springs, neaps or mid range?

b) During the early morning of Friday 25 May? Is it springs, neaps or mid range?

c) During the afternoon of Friday 29 June? Is it springs, neaps or mid range?

8.6

At Cherbourg on the evening of Thursday 17 May, the LW height is 0.9m and the HW is at 2117 BST, 6.5m. Calculate the height of tide 3½hrs before HW.

8.7

What is the height of tide at Cherbourg 4hrs after HW on the morning of Wednesday 8 August?

8.8

a) What will be the height of tide at St Helier at 1057 BST on Wednesday 29 August?

b) With this height of tide, how much water will there be under the keel of a boat with a draught of 2.0m as it passes over a 3.5m drying height?

8.9

At 1740 BST on Sunday 24 June, the skipper of a motor cruiser arrives at his overnight anchorage near St Helier.

a) What is the height of tide at 1740?

b) By how much will the tide fall between 1740 and the next LW?

c) The boat has a draught of 1.2m and the skipper wants at least 1m under the keel at LW. What is the minimum depth in which to anchor to give this clearance?

8.10

At 2100 BST on Saturday 2 June a skipper picks up a mooring near St Malo for the night. The depth of water at the mooring is 12.0m at 2100 and the draught of the yacht is 1.8m. What will the clearance under the keel be at LW?

Please monsieur! Which way is north?

9 Safety

9.1

You have invited friends, who are novice sailors, to spend the day with you on the boat. What general advice would you give them regarding clothing and equipment to bring with them?

9.2

Your 10m boat has an engine, three separate cabins and a saloon area. How many fire extinguishers should you fit and where should they be placed?

9.3

Boatowners are advised to have a gas tap fitted close to the cooker or a solenoid at the gas bottle. Why is this?

9.4

Your intended cruising area is within 5 miles of the coast. Which type of flare pack would you be advised to carry?

9.5

When might it be beneficial to use an LED flare?

9.6

Give four basic safety rules that would help prevent accidents when using a dinghy to go ashore from a moored boat.

Launching the dinghy. Photo: Alamy.

9.7

Which of the following would you consider suitable as attachment points for a safety harness line?

a) Running rigging

b) Standing rigging

c) Webbing jackstays

d) Guardrail wires

e) The mast

9.8

As a responsible boatowner you join the RYA SafeTrx. What sort of information will you be uploading and who has access?

9.9

Which of the following should NOT be discharged into the sea from a boat afloat?

a) In the marina:

   i) marine toilet

   ii) washing-up water

   iii) trash

   iv) banana skin and apple core

b) Two miles off the coast:

   i) marine toilet

   ii) drink cans and plastic bottles

   iii) scrapings from a saucepan

   iv) oily bilge water

9.10

You have a casualty aboard and the SAR helicopter is being sent to evacuate him to hospital. How should you prepare your boat and the crew for the arrival of the helicopter?

10 Rules of the Road

10.1
Do the Rules for Preventing Collisions at Sea give one vessel 'right of way' over another?

10.2
What does the flag in Figure 10.1 indicate?

What action should an approaching vessel take?

Fig 10.1 *Boat displaying a signal flag.*

10.3
The Rules require all vessels to maintain a lookout at all times. What factors may hinder the keeping of a good lookout?

10.4
How can the skipper assess whether a risk of collision exists with another vessel?

10.5

Complete the following sentences:

a) In a narrow channel, vessels should keep to the .... side of the channel.

b) Vessels under 20m in length and sailing vessels should not ....

10.6

a) What fog signal should be sounded by an 11m power-driven vessel that is making way through the water?

b) What fog signal should be sounded by a sailing vessel under way?

c) How often should the signals in a) and b) be sounded?

10.7

What types of vessel show the lights featured in Figure 10.2? Which aspect is shown?

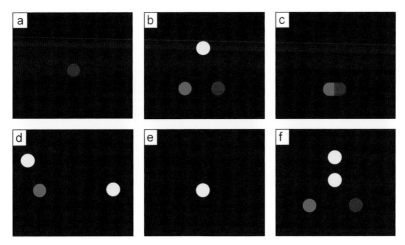

Fig 10.2 *Lights displayed by vessels.*

EXERCISES

10.8

The illustrations in Figure 10.3 show situations where a risk of collision exists.

Which is the 'give-way' vessel and what action should the skipper take?

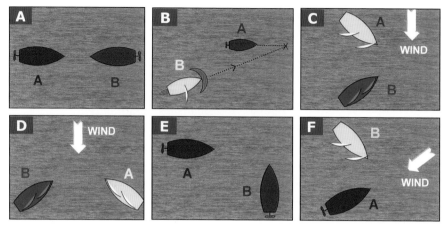

Fig 10.3 *Situations in which there is a collision risk.*

10.9

Under what circumstances would you display these day shapes?

Fig 10.4 *Day shapes.*

10.10

A yacht has been sailing at night using the tricolour light at the top of the mast. On approaching the destination, the sails are lowered and the engine is started. Should there be a change of lights? If so, what lights should be shown?

EXERCISES

11 Pilotage

Use the Stanfords Channel Islands chart and *Reeds Nautical Almanac* extracts at the back of the book for this exercise. Variation 3°W.

11.1
A skipper is on passage from Guernsey to Alderney in good visibility. He intends to use the Swinge channel and wishes to pass to the east of the Pierre au Vraic rock (to the south-west of the island).

a) How could he use Burhou Island to avoid the rock?

b) How could he check that he has passed the danger?

11.2
You are the skipper of a boat approaching Diélette (49° 33'N 001° 52'W) from the south-west. As the power station comes abeam, the light on the breakwater becomes visible. Describe the characteristics of the light you see.

11.3
A boat, leaving the bay (near the TV mast) on the north coast of Jersey at night, is using the leading lights in transit astern in order to remain clear of any off-lying dangers. The helmsman loses concentration for a moment and the lights separate as shown in Figure 11.1.

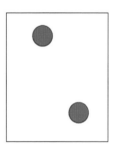

a) Should the helmsman alter course to port or to starboard to bring the lights back in line?

Fig 11.1 *Lights.*

b) How could the skipper use the light on Sorel Point to make sure that he passes clear to the west of Les Dirouilles on his way north-eastwards to Diélette?

11.4
The navigator of a 12m motor cruiser is planning a daylight entry into St Peter Port (Guernsey) from the north. Use extract 12 to answer the following:

a) How could he make sure that he is on a safe course from Roustel beacon to the harbour entrance?

b) As the boat approaches the harbour, he sees a fixed red light displayed from White Rock Pier head. May the boat enter the harbour?

c) What dangers are there in the harbour area?

d) On which VHF channel could the skipper call the marina?

e) The boat enters the harbour 4hrs before HW and the skipper decides that he will refuel before berthing in Victoria Marina. Where should he berth to get fuel? Is diesel fuel available at all times?

f) What is the speed limit in the harbour?

g) The height of HW St Peter Port is 7.0m. When is there access to the marina for a 1.5m draught boat?

h) How is entry into Victoria marina controlled?

11.5

You are sailing with friends and have just completed your first cross-channel passage. It is still daylight on a fine evening as the boat approaches Cherbourg from the north and the skipper asks you whether you would like to prepare a pilotage plan for entry into the harbour's western entrance and for berthing in the marina. The boat draws 1.7m.

a) Which publications should you gather together for the task?

b) The Stanfords chart has been used for the approaches to Cherbourg and now you intend to change to *Reeds Nautical Almanac* charts for the large-scale plan of the harbour (see extracts section). What adjustments must you make to the GNSS when switching to the *Almanac* charts?

c) Are there any restrictions or dangers within the harbour?

d) Are there any depth restraints within the marina area?

e) Which marina pontoons are available for visitors?

f) If there is a need to call the marina on the radio, which channel should be used?

g) Make a sketch plan of the harbour that you could use on deck for the harbour entry. On it, draw tracks and distances from Fort de l'Ouest to the marina entrance and features such as buoys and prominent landmarks. Show whether these features should be left to port or to starboard.

12 Aids to Navigation and Passage Planning

Use Stanfords Channel Islands chart and 3°W variation. All times are given in BST and answers should be in BST. Use tidal and port information from the back of the book.

Aids to navigation

12.1

When referring to a through-hull paddle wheel log, which of the following statements is true and which is false? Give reasons for your answer.

a) A log that under-reads is more dangerous than a log that over-reads.

b) The paddle wheel should be painted with anti-fouling paint to prevent barnacle build-up.

c) The log measures speed and distance run through the water, not the speed over the ground.

d) When the boat is not being used, the paddle wheel should be removed and the blanking plug put in its place.

12.2

Depth sounders may be set to read:

a) Depth below the keel.

b) Depth below the waterline.

c) Depth below the transducer.

What are the advantages or disadvantages of each setting?

12.3

The GNSS usually gives a position that is accurate to the nearest 15m for 95 per cent of the time. Suggest three reasons why the signal could be adversely affected.

Passage planning

When planning a passage, remember that the International SOLAS rules legally require that a passage plan is made and that the following points (as a minimum) should be considered:

- weather
- navigational hazards
- condition of vessel
- tidal height/stream
- crew ability
- contingency plans

12.4

You are planning a passage from St Malo to Granville in a 10m yacht in June. The yacht cruises at 6kn and the weather forecast is for fair weather and a SW3 wind. HW St Helier is at 1317 BST (neaps). HW St Malo is at 1300 BST. HW Granville is at 1303 BST. Use information from extracts 16 and 17 to answer the following:

a) When is there access to the Hérel marina at Granville?

b) What is the distance from the marina in St Malo to Granville?

c) Approximately how long will the passage take at 6kn? (Exclude tidal stream.)

d) Using diamond ⟨R⟩, at what time does the stream become favourable for the passage?

e) Is exit from Les Bas-Sablons marina at St Malo possible at the time the stream becomes favourable?

f) At what time would you leave St Malo?

Yachts in harbour dressed overall.

12.5

You are about halfway on the passage to Granville when the weather deteriorates unexpectedly and the wind freshens from the west.

a) What should you do? Go on, go back or seek shelter? Give reasons.

b) If you decide to seek shelter, where could you safely go?

12.6

You are planning to make a daylight passage from the outer harbour at St Peter Port, Guernsey to the marina in St Helier, Jersey in your 10m yacht on Thursday 30 August. The boat has a draught of 1.7m and an average cruising speed of 5.5kn in smooth water. The weather forecast is westerly force 3 to 4, slight sea and good visibility.

a) What is the approximate distance from St Peter Port to St Helier?

b) What is the time of HW Dover during daylight? Is it neaps or springs?

c) Using the tidal stream atlas (extracts 2A and 2B), at what time does the stream begin running southward towards Jersey? At what time does it become unfavourable along the south coast of Jersey?

d) If the average speed of favourable tide is 2.0kn what will be the approximate passage time?

e) What is the time of HW St Helier on the evening of the 30 August?

f)   When is there access to St Helier marina during the evening?

g) At what time will you leave St Peter Port?

h) Make an outline plan to include waypoints, prominent landmarks and hazards.

13 Weather

13.1
Complete the following sentence:

A strong wind warning is issued when winds of force .... are expected.

13.2
If Beaufort force 8 were forecast, which of the following could be expected?

a) 28–33kn   b) 34–40kn   c) 41–47kn

13.3
What is the meaning of the following terms, when used in weather forecasts?

a) Sea state moderate   c) Soon

b) Poor visibility   d) Backing

13.4
HM Coastguard broadcasts maritime safety information on marine VHF.

a) Which VHF channel will be used to announce these broadcasts?

b) Will they be made:

    i) hourly?   iii) four hourly?

    ii) three hourly?   iv) six hourly?

13.5
Looking at Figure 13.1, which number corresponds to the feature in the list below?

a) Centre of high pressure   g) Showers

b) Cold front   h) Anticlockwise winds

c) Light and variable winds   i) Warm front

d) Occluded front   j) High cirrus cloud

e) Clockwise winds   k) Centre of low pressure

f) Poor visibility

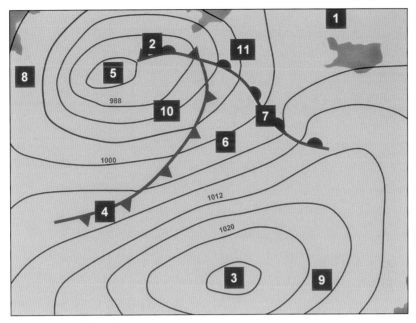

Fig 13.1 *Weather chart.*

13.6
Which of the following cloud types (Fig 13.2) would you find at position 10 in Figure 13.1?

Fig 13.2 *Types of cloud.*

13.7
You have decided to make a passage westward along the coast in a fast motor cruiser that planes well at 25kn. The wind is forecast to be westerly force 4 and it is a spring tide. Will you go when the tidal stream is against you or with you? Give reasons.

13.8
Use the Stanford Channel Island chart to suggest a sheltered anchorage off Sark in strong south-westerly winds.

13.9

On fine summer days, the weather is calm during the morning but the wind increases and changes direction by afternoon. Why is this? Use the diagram in Figure 13.3 to illustrate what is happening.

Fig 13.3 *Blank template for 13.9.*

13.10

When anchored close to a sheltered shore in a mountainous region, what may happen to the wind strength overnight?

14 Communications

14.1

Two vessels with 16m-high antennas are closing each other. At what distance will they first be able make contact using a VHF marine radio?

a) 80 miles

c) 16 miles

b) 35 miles

d) 3 miles

Choose one answer.

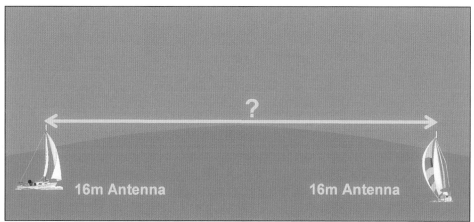

Fig 14.1 *Diagram of the scenario in 14.1.*

14.2

What is the purpose of the squelch control on the radio:

a) To limit background hiss?

b) To reduce the power of transmissions?

c) To save the boat's batteries?

14.3

Which VHF channel is used for distress working and for general calling?

14.4

The motor cruiser *Flamingo* has a serious fire in the engine space, which the crew are unable to extinguish. The skipper decides to send a distress alert and message before he and the two crew members abandon to the liferaft with the hand-held VHF radio. The GNSS position is 49° 52'.43N 006°12'.35W. The callsign and MMSI are ZQM3 and 235899986.

a) For how long should he keep the red button depressed when sending a digital distress alert?

b) What information is sent digitally when the distress alert is sent?

c) Looking at the first three figures of the MMSI in Figure 14.2, what nationality is *Flamingo*?

d) Write down the distress message the skipper will send by voice.

14.5
Which of the following transmissions is strictly forbidden?

a) Swearing and abusive language.

b) Calls to a UK Coastguard using Ch 67.

c) Playing music.

Fig 14.2 *Standard Horizon GX2200E Matrix AIS/GPS radio.*

14.6
Which of the following is NOT an inter-ship channel?

a) 72   b) 03   c) 06   d) 77

14.7
Which channel would you expect yacht club safety boats to use?

a) Ch M2   b) Ch 80   c) Ch M1

14.8
To which authority should you apply for a ship's radio licence?

14.9
Give the phonetic for each of the following letters:

a) C   b) H   c) M   d) N   e) R   f) V   g) Y

14.10
When you have finished a conversation with another boat, should you finish with the words?

a) Over   b) Over and out   c) Ciao   d) Out

15 The Diesel Engine

15.1

Which letter in Figure 15.1 corresponds to each of the following?

i)   Starter motor   ii) Drive belt   iii) Alternator   iv) Water pump

v) Coolant cap   vi) Fuses   vii) Gear box   viii) Impeller housing

Fig 15.1 *Parts of the diesel engine.*

15.2

With reference to the operation of the diesel engine, what is meant by the following terms?

a) Suck   b) Squeeze   c) Bang   d) Blow

15.3

Certain daily checks are necessary to keep a diesel engine in good running order.

How should the following be checked?

a) Drive belt   b) Oil   c) Sea water filter   d) Coolant

15.4

Complete the following sentence:

The fuel needs to be free of i) .... ii) .... iii) .... to facilitate smooth running.

15.5

Why is it considered inadvisable for amateur mechanics to service injectors and the fuel injection pump?

15.6

Are the following statements true or false?

The engine should:

a) always be run at low revs

b) be fully warmed before stopping

c) be in gear and under load when charging the batteries alongside

d) always started with full throttle

e) be stopped by pulling the 'Engine (fuel) stop lever'

f) be stopped by turning the power switch off

15.7

The components in Figure 15.2 are all parts of the fuel system of a small marine diesel. Place the parts in the correct order.

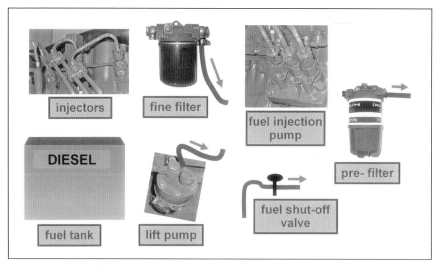

Fig 15.2 *Parts of the fuel system.*

16 General

16.1
What is the meaning of the following chart symbols?

a)   **b)**   **c)**   **d)**

Fig TP1.1

16.2
What is the depth of water in the following positions if the height of tide has been calculated as 3.2m?

a) 48° 34'.6N 002° 44'.8W

b) 153°T from Cap Fréhel lighthouse 3.0M

16.3
What is the latitude and longitude of Cap Fréhel lighthouse?

16.4
Use the Dover tide table and tidal stream charts in the Almanac section.

What is the direction and rate of the tidal stream on the south-west corner of Guernsey between 0153 and 0253 BST on Friday 31 August?

16.5
a) What knot is shown in Figure TP1.2? Why is this a good knot to use when securing a line to the pillar of a cleat or to a ring?

b) How would you describe the type of rope used?

Fig TP1.2

16.6

A skipper is planning a passage westward, with the tidal stream, from St Malo to Dahouet.

a) The weather forecast is giving SE5. What sea state could he expect close inshore?

b) If the wind were to veer, would it become:
   i) north-easterly OR ii) south-westerly?

c) Would either of the wind directions mentioned in 16.6b cause him to change his plans? Give reasons.

16.7

a) What type of buoy is shown in Figure TP1.3?

b) What is the colour of the light?

c) What is the characteristic of the light?

d) Should the buoy be left to the west or to the east?

16.8

The yacht *Hole-in-One* is in position 48° 45'.0N 001° 40'.0W when it hits an underwater object and begins to take in water rapidly. The skipper tells his three crew that the boat will soon sink and he prepares to send a distress alert and a distress message on the radio. The crew prepare the liferaft ready for abandonment.

Fig TP1.3

a) The radio, a VHF-DSC (Callsign GB2a, MMSI 235899986), has a red button under a protective cover. It is interfaced with the GNSS set. For how long should the skipper press this button?

b) What information is sent with the digital data signal?

c) Write the VHF voice message sent by the skipper.

16.9

A risk of collision exists between the vessels in Figure TP1.4.

For each picture, nominate the 'give-way' vessel and state what action it should take.

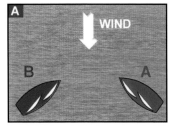
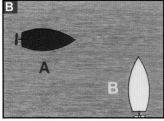
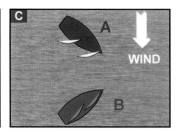

Fig TP1.4

16.10

What type of vessel is indicated (Figure TP1.5) by each set of lights? Mention aspect and length.

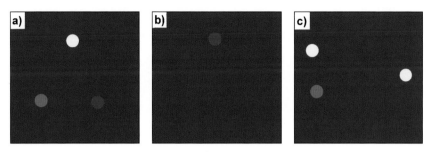

Fig TP1.5

16.11

a) What is the fog signal for a power-driven vessel making way through the water?

b) What is the fog signal for a yacht under sail?

16.12

What day shape should be shown by a vessel at anchor?

17 General

17.1

a) What is the name of the knot (or bend) shown in Figure TP2.1?

b) For what purpose would you use such a knot?

17.2

What type of rope would be most suitable for:

a) Halyards?

b) A line thrown to a casualty in the water?

c) Anchor warp?

Fig TP2.1

17.3

What is the meaning of the following chart symbols?

Fig TP2.2

17.4

What is the latitude and longitude of Casquets Lighthouse, which lies approximately 5 miles to the west of Alderney?

17.5

What is the depth of water in the following positions if the height of tide is 4.3m?

a) 49° 35'.40N 001° 50'.08W.

b) 280°T from the 279m chimney on the north-west corner of the Cherbourg Peninsula, distance 2.4M.

17.6

a) What type of buoy is shown in Figure TP2.3?

b) What is the colour of the light?

c) If the top mark were missing from the buoy how would it be possible to determine what type of buoy it is?

d) Your boat is heading 270°M when you see the buoy in Figure TP2.3 dead ahead. Should you alter course to port or to starboard?

Fig TP2.3

17.7

What precautions should be taken when using the dinghy?

17.8

A risk of collision exits between the vessels shown in Figure TP2.4.

For each picture, nominate the 'give-way' vessel and state what action it should take.

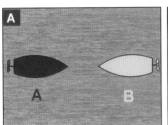 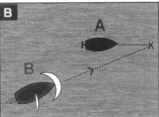 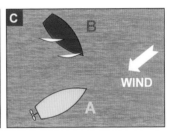

Fig TP2.4

17.9

What type of vessel is indicated by each set of lights in Figure TP2.5?

Mention aspect and length.

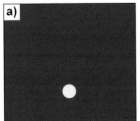  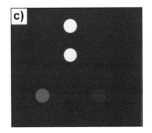

Fig TP2.5

GENERAL

17.10
How can you assess whether a risk of collision exists with another vessel?

17.11
a) When is a strong wind warning issued by the Met Office?

b) When is a gale warning issued?

17.12
Your motor cruiser *Firebrand*, with three people aboard, suffers a serious engine fire that cannot be extinguished. You send a distress alert and distress message over the radio and then prepare to abandon to the liferaft. What preparations would you make and what instructions will you give to your crew?

The skipper will brief the crew on safety procedures.

18 Chartwork

All times are in BST; answers to be given in BST. Use the tidal diamonds for questions 2 and 3. Use St Helier tide tables and tidal curve (Extracts 3 and 4) for question 4. Use 3°W variation.

18.1

At 0800, the following bearings were taken by a navigator north-east of St Malo.

Monument on headland	166°M
East cardinal beacon	206°M
Rochefort beacon	238°M
Log reads	7.9M (miles)

Plot the three-point fix and give the latitude and longitude.

18.2

A motor cruiser is at South Minquiers cardinal mark at 1736 on Wednesday 15 August.

a) What is the magnetic course to steer to the safe water mark in the approaches to St Malo with a boat speed of 24kn?

b) Approximately how long will the passage take?

c) What is the speed over the ground?

d) What will be the magnetic course to steer to counteract 10° leeway in a fresh breeze from the west?

18.3

A yacht navigator has entered a waypoint at the centre of the compass rose to make position fixing easier. At 1135 BST on Saturday 16 June, the GNSS gives the bearing and distance to the centre of the compass rose to the north-east of St Malo as 060°T, 4.6M. The helmsman is steering 185°M, his best course to windward. The average speed is 6kn.

a) What is the latitude and longitude at 1135?

b) If the yacht continues on this course will it pass safely to the west of Grand Jardin lighthouse (near St Malo entrance)?

c) What is the true course over the ground?

18.4

At 1704 BST on Saturday 9 June, a skipper drops anchor in a depth of 5.0m off St Helier, Jersey. He wonders whether the depth is sufficient to give him a clearance of 1.5m under the keel at the next low water.

a) His first task is to calculate the height of tide at the time of anchoring. What will his answer be?

b) By how much will the tide fall between the answer to a) and the next LW height?

c) If the draught of the boat is 2.0m, will the clearance be sufficient at the next LW or should the skipper consider re-laying the anchor in deeper water?

A snug berth in St Peter Port.

19 Chartwork

All times are in BST; answers to be given in BST. Use St Helier tide tables and tidal curves (Extracts 3 and 4) for question 4. Use 3°W variation.

19.1

The skipper of a boat on passage from Guernsey to Sark takes the following bearings at 1100 on Monday 23 July:

Roustel beacon in transit with Brehon Tower   021°M

South cardinal mark with bell   114°M

Log reads   1.2M (miles)

Plot the fix and give the latitude and longitude.

19.2

Continuing from question 19.1, the boat arrives at the south cardinal mark (with bell) at 1130.

a) What is the magnetic course to steer to the anchorage in La Grande Grève on the west coast of Sark with a boat speed of 5kn? Use diamond ◇F◇ from the tidal stream table at the bottom of the chart.

NB Remember the diamond table is based on HW St Helier.

b) What is the speed over the ground?

c) Approximately how long will it take to reach the anchorage?

d) If there were 5° of leeway due to a breeze from the north-east, what magnetic course should the helmsman now steer to counteract it?

19.3

At 1339 BST the following information is entered into the log book of a motor cruiser.

Position: 49° 24'.0N 002° 15'.7W

Average speed: 18kn

Course steered: 275°M

Tidal stream: 200°T 4.4kn

a) Plot the estimated position for 1409.

b) Will this heading clear the tide rips off Sark?

c) What is the true course over the ground?

19.4

It is 2150 BST on Thursday 17 May. A skipper is about to anchor for the night close to St Helier in Jersey and does not wish to go aground overnight. The boat draws 1.2m and he would like to have a 2.0m clearance under the boat at low water.

a) What is the height of the tide at the time of anchoring?

b) How much will the tide fall between 2150 and low water?

c) What is the minimum depth of water in which to anchor to give the required clearance?

Starboard hand Platte Rock marker, Guernsey.

1 Seamanship and Ropework

1.1a

1) M	5) T	9) C	13) F	17) A
2) E	6) B	10) L	14) R	18) S
3) N	7) D	11) H	15) J	19) G
4) P	8) Q	12) I	16) O	20) K

Fig A1.1a *Question 1.1a.*

1.1b

1) K	5) H	9) N	13) J	17) O
2) G	6) A	10) L	14) E	
3) M	7) D	11) I	15) C	
4) P	8) F	12) Q	16) B	

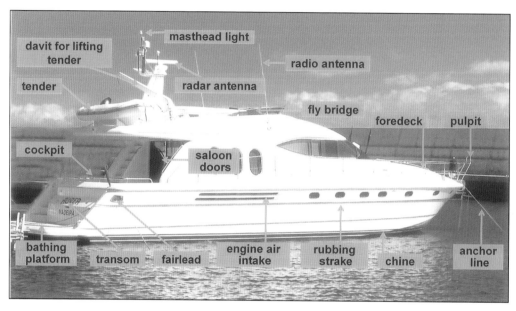

Fig. A1.1b *Question 1.1b.*

1.2

1) C	2) A	3) B

1.3

1) B	2) A	3) C

1.4

A is a bowline.
The bowline is a knot used for making a temporary non-slip loop in the end of a rope. It may be slipped over a cleat or bollard for shore lines or may be tied around the waist as a rescue line.

B is a clove hitch.
This hitch is for securing fenders to the guard rail and for securing a tiller amidships.

C is a figure-of-eight knot.
The figure-of-eight is tied in the end of a rope as a stopper knot. This prevents the rope running out through a block.

1.5

The names of the lines are shown in Figure A1.2.

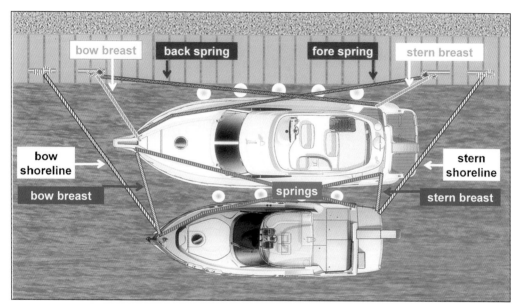

Fig A1.2 *Question 1.5.*

1.6

A = Bruce   B = CQR (Plough)   C = Delta

1.7

Any five from:

a) Shelter from the wind, both current and forecast.

b) Good holding ground. Sand and mud are good, provided that there is no kelp lying over the sand. Shells, gravel and rock are not ideal for any of the anchors shown in question 1.6.

c) Away from prohibited areas, ie power and telephone cables.

d) Out of a busy channel.

e) Sufficient swinging room.

f) Sufficient depth of water at LW.

g) Out of strong tidal stream or current.

h) Close to a landing place.

i) Suitable for an exit in the dark, ie no unmarked rocks on the route.

1.8

Anchor warp should be made of nylon because it is extremely strong and stretches, so reducing snubbing. Multi-plait is very pliable and does not kink.

1.9

a) 28m.

b) 42m.

1.10

a) The red ensign, which should be flown at all times when under way in territorial waters (except when racing) and between 0800 in summer (0900 in winter) and sunset when in harbour.

b) A burgee, which usually carries the emblem of a yacht club and is hoisted on members' boats.

c) A courtesy ensign – the national maritime flag of the country being visited.

A British ensign is flown from the stern.

2 Introduction to Chartwork

2.1
Most GNSS receivers default to the international datum, WGS 84. When using a chart based on an alternative datum, it is necessary to select 'datums' from the 'set-up' menu so that the correct datum may be entered. Failing to do this may result in errors of up to 200m in the given position.

2.2
The orange colouring depicts the area that is uncovered with water at chart datum.

2.3
a) A dangerous wreck.

b) Radio mast.

c) A restricted area.

d) A rock, depth unknown, considered dangerous. Depth less than 2m on Stanford chart.

2.4
10m. The paler blue shading shows water less than 10m.

2.5
With Mercator projection, the parallels of latitude are spaced increasingly further apart as the distance from the equator increases. It is therefore necessary to measure distance level with the vessel's position.

2.6
a) SW and ii) 225°.

b) E and vii) 090°.

c) NW and vi) 315°.

d) W and v) 270°.

e) N and i) 000°.

f) SE and iii) 135°.

g) NE and viii) 045°.

h) S and iv) 180°.

2.7

a) 49° 10'.8N 002° 14'.9W

b) 48° 38'.2N 001° 30'.6W

c) 48° 58'.9N 002° 07'.4W

2.8

a) Tidal diamond Q.

b) The nature of the sea bed: sand, broken shells.

c) Safe water mark.

2.9

Anchoring is prohibited because there is a power cable extending offshore.

2.10

Admiralty Notices to Mariners, which may be downloaded from the UKHO website free of charge. Yachting magazines such as *Practical Boat Owner* also publish notices relevant to small craft.

The Needles, Isle of Wight.

3 Buoys, Beacons and Lights

3.1

a) This is an east cardinal mark (Men-Marc'h), that marks the eastern side of an area of rocks. The yacht should pass to the east of the buoy. The top mark has two black triangles with bases together and the main buoy is coloured black, yellow and black.

Fig A3.1

b) An isolated danger mark that can be passed on either side. It has two black balls as a top mark and the buoy is painted in black, red, black horizontal bands (see Figure A3.1).

c) A starboard hand mark, similar to the one in question 3.2a.

3.2

a) A green light, any sequence.

b) A red light, any sequence.

c) A white light, quick flashing or very quick flashing in groups of nine.

3.3

a) A white and red sectored light, flashing in groups of three every ten seconds.

b) 15m above MHWS.

c) It has a nominal range of 14 nautical miles.

d) The horn gives three blasts every 30 seconds.

3.4

In the red sector.

3.5

No, the light is obscured in that position.

3.6

a) This is a temporary buoy used to mark a wreck until permanent buoys can be placed.

b) 3.) The light is alternating blue and yellow.

3.7

- An *isophase* light has equal periods of light and dark, eg on for four seconds and off for four seconds.

- A *flashing* light has a period of darkness that is longer than its period of light.

- An *occulting* light has longer periods of light than periods of darkness.

3.8

a) A safe water mark sometimes known as a 'fairway' or mid-channel buoy. They can be passed on either side, although by convention they should be kept on your port hand. That way you will always be favouring the starboard hand side of the channel.

b) To starboard.

c) To port.

d) To port.

e) To starboard.

3.9

Beacon A should be placed at the junction.

3.10

It should be red in colour and conical in shape (see Figure A3.2).

Fig A3.2

4 Compass and Position Fixing

4.1

The variation was 4° 05' W in 1997. This error is decreasing about 7mins annually. It is 11 years since 1997 so 77mins have to be deducted from 4° 05' W.

77mins = 1° 17'

4° 05' W less 1° 17' = 2° 48' W. Practically, the variation used will be rounded up to the nearest whole degree, ie 3°W.

4.2

True to magnetic:

a) 235°T + 3°W = 238°M

b) 356°T + 7°W = 003°M

c) 135°T − 9°E = 126°M

d) 002°T − 11°E = 351°M

4.3

Magnetic to true:

a) 285°M − 3°W = 282°T

b) 004°M − 5°W = 359°T

c) 207°M + 6°E = 213°T

d) 357°M + 5°E = 002°T

4.4

A number of items on the boat cause deviation, the combination of which gives the boat its own polarity. This deviation will alter with the ship's heading. Possible causes include:

a) Magnetic influences from some analogue navigational instruments, magnets in outboard, motors stored on board and magnets in loudspeakers of radios and mobile phones.

b) Ferromagnetic influences from iron and mild steel objects such as the engine, keel, some food cans, hand-held flares, some anchors and batteries.

c) Electromagnetic influences from wire carrying electric current and aerial feeder cables.

4.5

The Chenal de la Petite Porte leading line is shown as 130°T. The variation is 3°W, which means that the compass should read 133°M as the boat heads down the line. However, the compass reads 135°C. This is greater than it should be so we can apply the useful rhyme:

'If the compass reads best (greater) then the deviation is WEST'

So the deviation on a heading of 133°M = 2°W.

4.6

The leading line into St Helier is charted as 023°T.

Variation is 3°W so the compass should read 026°M. In reality it reads 020°C which gives a 6° error. So we apply the rhyme:

'If the compass reads least then the deviation is EAST'

Therefore deviation is 6°E on a heading of 026°M.

4.7

49° 43'.2N 001° 30'.8W. Also see Figure A4.1.

The depth sounder reading has been taken to help confirm the position. Depths inshore of the 0530 position are less and to seaward they are greater, so the 42m depth is reasonable.

4.8

49° 42'.0N 001° 36'.9W. Also see Figure A4.1.

4.9

See plot in Figure A4.1. This position is unreliable because of the narrow angle of cut between the two bearings. A small error in either of the bearings will give a large area of uncertainty.

4.10

49° 43'.9N 001° 48'.3W. See plot in Figure A4.1.

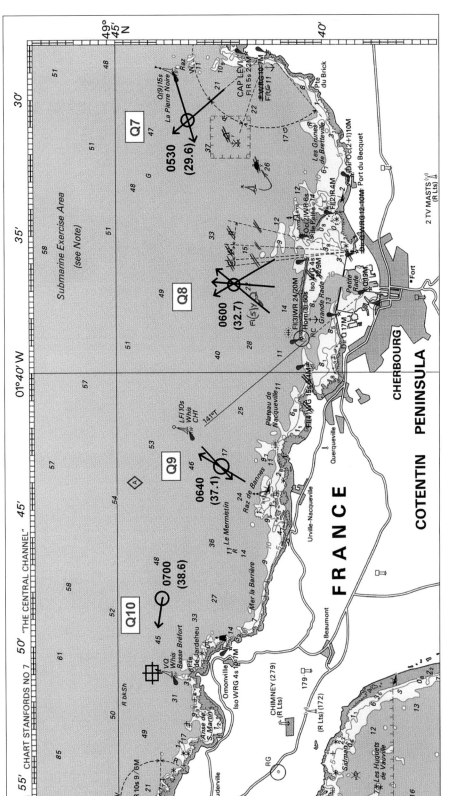

Fig A4.1 *Plot for questions 4.7 to 4.10.*

5 Tidal Streams

5.1

a) 030°T   2.2kn, neap rate

b) 213°T   2.4kn, spring rate

c) 116°T   0.3kn

Take an average of the St Helier spring and neap rates to calculate the mid-range rate.

5.2

Between 0800 and 0900. The 'HW hour' is calculated as being 30mins either side of the HW time.

Stream on Lepe Spit buoy in the Solent.

5.3

HW St Helier is at 1400. The HW hour is 1330–1430.

Departure time is at 1730 so the tidal hour to use is 1730–1830 = HW +4hrs.

5.4

a)   **Wednesday 16 May:**

 HW St Helier 0542 UT +1hr for BST = 0642. Range 9.7m, springs

The HW hour = 0612–0712. Direction and rate = 054°T 0.6kn.

b)   **Sunday 24 June:**

HW St Helier 1320 UT +1hr for BST = 1420. Range 4.0m, neaps

The HW hour = 1350–1450

HW +2hrs = 1550–1650. Direction and rate = 289°T 0.9kn.

c)   **Sunday 5 August:**

HW St Helier 1037 UT +1hr = 1137 BST. Range 7.8m, mid range

The HW hour = 1107–1207 BST

HW –3hrs = 0807–0907. Direction and rate = 107°T 2.5kn.

5.5

Dover.

5.6

a) 102°T 0.4kn.

b) 236°T 5.0kn.

c) 318°T Spring rate = 1.1kn neap rate = 0.5kn. Mid range rate = 0.8kn.

5.7

a) **Thursday 17 May:**

HW Dover 1205 BST 6.7m. LW 0.8m. Range 5.9m, springs. HW hour = 1135–1235

Time required 1335–1435 = HW +2hrs = 287°T 3.5kn.

b) **Sunday 24 June:**

HW Dover 1913 BST 5.4m. LW 2.2m. Range 3.2m, neaps. HW hour 1843–1943

Time required 1443–1543 = HW –4hrs = 026°T 0.6kn.

c) **Saturday 28 July:**

HW Dover 2311 BST 6.0m. LW 1.5m. Range 4.5m, mid range. HW hour 2241–2341

Time required 2140–2240 = HW –1hr, neaps 1.7kn, springs 3.9, mid range 2.8kn

Direction and rate = 285°T 2.8kn.

The weak stream is just strong enough for the pick-up buoy to float downstream at Buckler's Hard.

5.8

Saturday 26 May:

HW Dover 2023 BST

HW hour = 1953–2053

Strongest stream at 4hrs before HW Dover

Tidal hour HW –4hrs = 1553–1653.

5.9

Tuesday 10 July:

HW Dover 0745 BST

Stream turns south-west at 0715 (at the beginning of the HW hour).

5.10

Wednesday 15 August:

HW Dover 1338 BST

HW hour is 1308–1408

Tidal stream is slack south of Jersey at HW +2hrs = 1508–1608.

6 Dead Reckoning and Estimated Position

6.1
DR position at 0940 = 49° 22'.2N 001° 55'.5W. See plot in Figure A6.1.

6.2
a) See plot in Figure A6.1.

b) Course over the ground is 090°T.

c) Speed over the ground is 7.5kn.

6.3
a) See plot in Figure A6.1. Position at 1330 = 49° 28'.3N 002° 12'.7W.

b) Speed over the ground is 5.4kn.

6.4
a) and b) See plot in Figure A6.1.

HW St Helier 2000. Springs. HW hour 1930–2030

Start time 1430.

HW –5hrs = 1430–1530 ⬦G 186°T 2.1kn, spring rate ½hr = 1.05M

c) 49° 23'.4N 002° 00'.5W.

A peaceful haven in the Baltic.

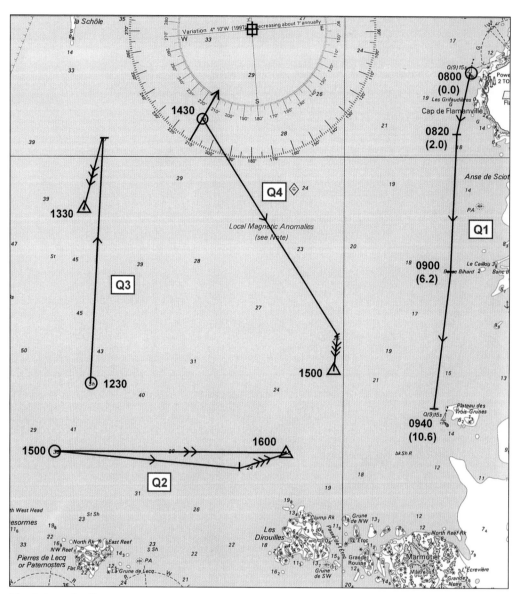

Fig A6.1 *Plot for questions 6.1 to 6.4.*

6.5

a) Subtract the 1653 log reading (10.1) from the 1753 reading (15.6) to get the distance travelled through the water = 5.5M.

b) **Wednesday 6 June:**

HW Dover 1523 BST. Range 4.6m. Mid range.

c) Course steered 160°M = 157°T

HW hour 1453–1553

Use the figures to the south of Sark.

HW +2hrs 1653–1753 = 240°T 1.3kn at neaps, 3.0kn at springs = 2.15kn at mid range.

d) 49° 15'.5N 002° 21'.2W. See plot in Figure A6.2.

e) SOG = 6.1kn. COG = 177°T.

6.6

a) See the plot in Figure A6.2.

Wednesday 4 July:

HW St Helier 0952 BST. Range 8.3m, springs

HW hour 0922–1022

⟨J⟩ HW –1hr = 0822–0922 063°T 2.2kn.

b) The yacht will sail too close to the reef for comfort so a tack will be necessary.

c) A clearing bearing could be drawn to Sorel Point lighthouse. The yacht must tack before the bearing becomes greater than 125°M.

6.7

Wednesday 29 August:

HW St Helier 0757 BST spring range

HW hour = 0727–0827

HW +1 = 0827–0927 045°T 2.0kn ½hr = 1.0M

HW +2 = 0927–1027 035°T 1.4kn

Courses steered: 1 140°M = 137°T 5.8M

                 2 212°M = 209°T 3.6M

                 3 175°M = 172°T 5.2M

EP 49° 14'.1N 002° 25'.0W. See plot in Figure A6.2.

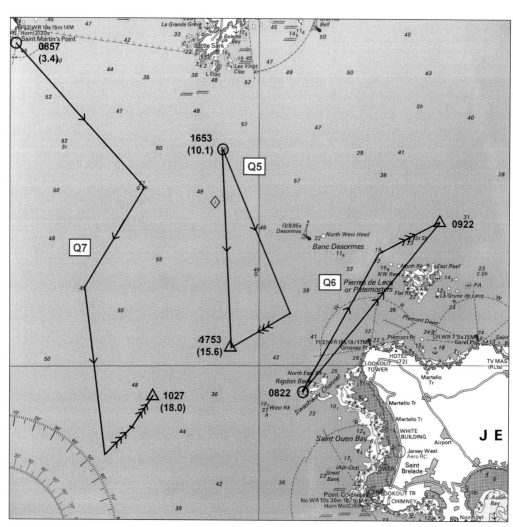

Fig A6.2 *Plot for questions 6.5 to 6.7.*

7 Course to Steer

7.1

See plot in Figure A7.1.

a) Course to steer is 019°T = 022°M.

b) Speed over the ground = 6.5kn.

7.2

See plot in Figure A7.1.

a) Course to steer is 201°T = 204°M.

b) SOG = 5.3kn.

c) Madeaux beacon will be seen on the starboard bow as the boat is actually on the line with two arrows but steering on 201°T.

7.3

See plot in Figure A7.1.

a) Use ½hr tide = 1.5M. Course to steer is 118°T = 121°M.

b) Speed over the ground = 31.0kn.

c) The passage will just over half an hour (around 32mins).

7.4

See plot in Figure A7.1.

a) Course to steer is 078°T = 081°M.

b) No, the boat will not remain directly on the track because allowance has been made for two different angles of tide. The boat should be slightly left of track during the first hour and will close the track in the second hour.

c) The skipper can keep a check on the amount of cross track error. It would be important to do this during this particular passage due to the proximity of the rocks on Plateau des Jaunes.

7.5

See plot in Figure A7.2.

a) **Thursday 23 August:**

HW St Helier 1438 BST. Neap range. HW hour 1408–1508

Time required 0908 onwards = HW –5hrs.   Stream 216°T, 2.5kn

Course to steer 188°T = 191°M.

b) SOG 8.4kn.

7.6

See plot in Figure A7.2.

a) **Friday 18 May:**

HW Dover 1250 BST. Range 5.9m, springs. HW hour 1220–1320

Time required 1420 = HW +2hrs 229°T, 2.2kn ½hr = 1.1M

Course to steer 269°T = 272°M.

b) Aim into the northerly wind to compensate for leeway. Course now 282°M.

7.7

See plot in Figure A7.2.

a) **Tuesday 5 June:**

HW St Helier 0954 BST. Range 6.8m Midway N/S

HW hour = 0924–1024

Ⓒ = HW +2hrs 1124–1224   349°T   3.0kn, springs 1.3kn neaps = 2.15 mid range

Ⓑ = HW +3hrs 1224–1324   033°T   2.3kn, springs 1.0kn neaps = 1.65 mid range

Course to steer: 048°T = 051°M.

b) Yes, the yacht should be clear of the overfalls.

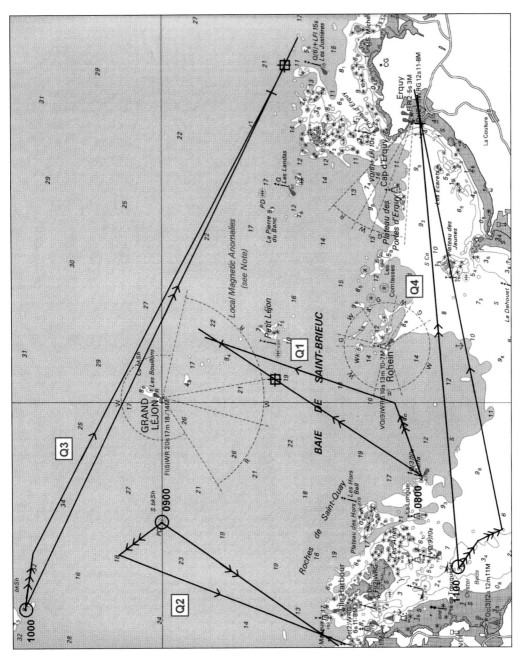

Fig A7.1 *Plot for questions 7.1 to 7.4.*

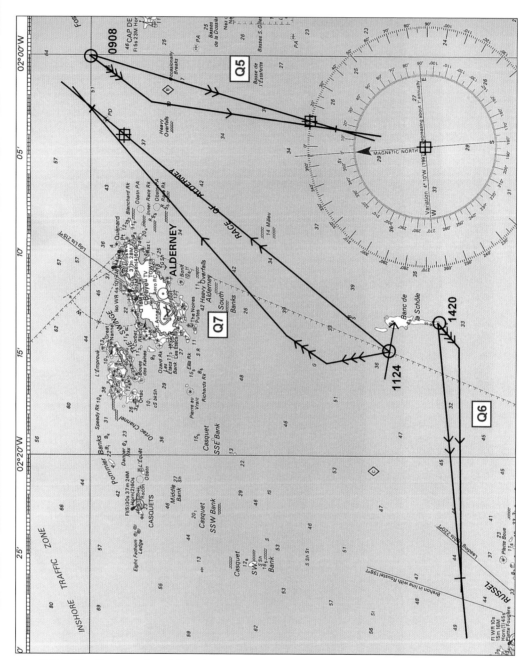

Fig A7.2 *Plot for questions 7.5 to 7.7.*

8 Tidal heights

8.1

i) A   iv) E   vii) D   x) G

ii) H   v) C   viii) J   xi) K

iii) B   vi) I   ix) F

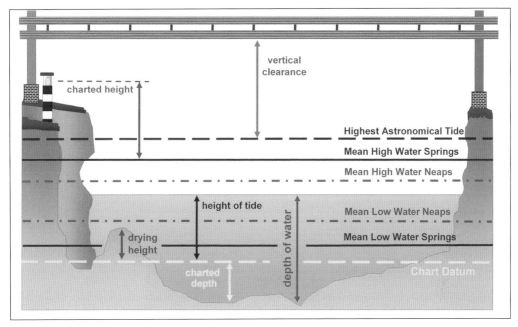

Fig A8.1 *Answer to question 8.1.*

8.2

a) Charted depth 3.5m + height of tide 3.0m = 6.5m.

b) Drying height −2.3m + height of tide 3.0m = 0.7m.

8.3

a) The anchorage is on the 5m contour + MHWS St Helier 11.0m = 16.0m.

b) MLWN St Helier =   4.0m

     Charted depth   =   drying   2.3m −

     Depth of water   =   1.7m

8.4

a) 0758 UT = 1hr for BST = 0858 BST 5.4m above chart datum.

b) 2055 UT + 1hr for BST = 2155 BST 11.1m.

c) 1339 BST 5.5m. *Note: The Cherbourg tide table is in French standard time, which is equal to British Summer Time.*

8.5

a) 11.1m. Springs.

b) 4.2m. Neaps.

c) 6.8m. Mid range.

8.6

As the curve for Cherbourg is based on HW we do not require the time of LW; just the height is entered on the lower left-hand side of the curve. The range is 5.6m, spring range, so we use the solid line on the curve for 3½hrs before HW.

The height of tide is 2.8m above datum at 1747 (3½hrs before 2117). See Figure A8.2.

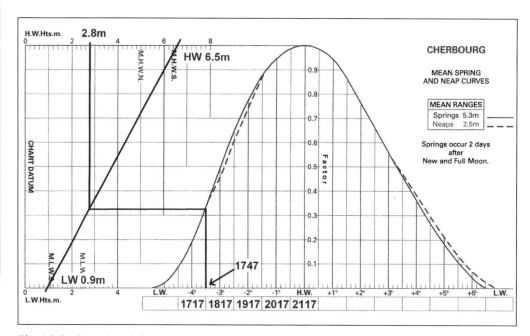

Fig A8.2 *Question 8.6.*

8.7

Cherbourg Wednesday 8 August:

HW 0355 5.0m. LW 2.5m. Range 2.5m neaps. We use the blue dotted line for neaps. The height of tide at 0755 is 3.5m above datum. See Figure A8.3 for the method.

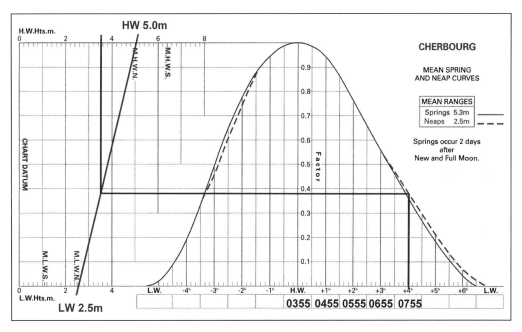

Fig A8.3 *Question 8.7.*

8.8

a) **St Helier Wednesday 29 August:**

HW 0757 BST 11.0m LW 1.1m. Range 9.9m, springs.

Enter the HW time in the box on the bottom line of the curve and fill in the subsequent boxes. 1057 is HW +3hrs. Height of tide = 6.6m.

b) There will be 1.1m under the keel at 1057. See Figure A8.4.

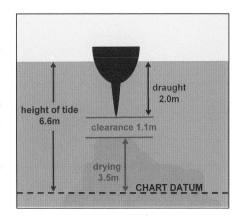

Fig A8.4 *Question 8.8b.*

8.9

a) **St Helier Sunday 24 June:**

HW 1420 8.0m LW 4.0m. Range 4.0m, neaps.

Height of tide at 1740 = 6.0m.

b) Height of tide 6.0m

LW height –4.0m

Fall to LW 2.0m between 1740 and LW.

c) See Figure A8.5.

8.10

St Malo Saturday 2 June:

HW 1959 11.4m LW (3 June) 2.4. Range 9.0m – close to spring range.

Using curve, height of tide is 10.9m at 2100 (HW + 1)

Fall to LW = 8.5m.

Add the draught and the fall to low water:

1.8m +8.5m = 10.3m

Now subtract 10.3m from the depth of water (12.0m) at the mooring at 2100.

Clearance under the keel at LW = 1.7m.

See Figure A8.6.

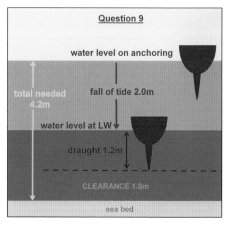

Fig A8.5 *Question 8.9c.*

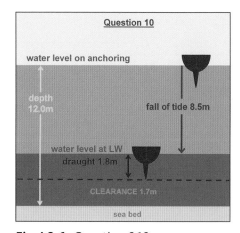

Fig A8.6 *Question 8.10.*

9 Safety

9.1

Your friends should bring a soft bag containing the following:

Sunscreen Use factor 40 or higher for good protection. The combination of sun, wind and salt spray means that skin burns very easily when at sea.

Sunglasses Reflected glare off the water can cause some eye damage in the long term so always wear good-quality sunglasses while on the water.

Shoes Soft-soled shoes that will grip on the deck. Trainers with white soles are usually acceptable.

Clothing Pack a woollen hat or a sun hat, a fleece and a windproof/waterproof jacket – it can get chilly in the cockpit or on the fly bridge. If possible they should also bring a change of clothing in case they get wet.

This sailor is well dressed for the occasion.

9.2

A fire extinguisher should be fitted in each of the cabins and in the saloon, four in all down below. A larger extinguisher for the engine should be stored in the cockpit locker or installed for automatic deployment in the engine space. In addition, it is advisable to have a fire blanket within reach of the cooking stove.

9.3

A gas tap should be installed near the cooker close to the termination of the rigid gas piping but before the rubber hose. Escaping gas is heavier than air and could sink into the bilge unnoticed if the rubber tubing were to split or chafe.

9.4

The coastal flare pack is supplied for craft venturing up to 7 miles from the coast. It contains:

- 2 × red parachute flares

- 2 × red hand-held flares

- 2 × orange hand-held smoke flares

The flares illustrated in Figure A9.1 are packed in a waterproof buoyant container.

Fig A9.1 *Pains Wessex coastal flare pack.*

9.5

Led flares are recommended to be carried in addition to conventional flares. They are much safer to use, especially in a liferaft, and are useful for a lifeboat or helicopter homing in on you as they 'burn' for many hours. They also have a longer shelf life but are not as efficient to attract attention initially.

9.6

i) Do not overload the boat and load it evenly – it should carry a label to indicate the maximum number of passengers.

ii) Take oars and spare fuel if using an outboard motor.

iii) Wear a lifejacket.

iv) Carry a waterproof bag containing:
- tools and a spark plug for the outboard
- hand-held VHF radio
- bailer
- pump
- torch (if returning after dark)

Zodiac Cadet inflatable. Photo: Avon Inflatables.

9.7

c – Webbing jackstays usually run the full length of the deck so that no re-clipping is required. It is strong if the stitching does not rot due to prolonged exposure to the sun; the webbing lies flat on the deck, unlike a wire jackstay, which rolls when trodden on.

e – The mast of a yacht would be a suitable attachment point when working at the mast and a short tether is required. You would be very unlucky if the mast were to fall down while you were attached!

9.8

The RYA SafeTrx is a free app that monitors your boat journeys and can alert emergency contacts should you fail to arrive on time. When an emergency contact calls HM Coastguard about an overdue trip, they will have access to your location and SafeTrx trip data.

All your vessels details, safety equipment and emergency contact numbers can be uploaded. Apart from yourself and the coastguard you can share the information with your friends and review passages. It's particularly useful when in mobile range and your vessel is not equipped with an AIS transceiver.

9.9

a) In the marina:
   i)   marine toilet
   iii) trash
   iv) banana skin and apple core

b) Two miles off the coast:
   i)   drink cans and plastic bottles
   iii) scrapings from a saucepan
   iv) oily bilge water

These are only guidelines for the UK. Many countries and inland waters have much stricter controls. Plastic should never be thrown over the side, including 'a message in a bottle'.

9.10

- Secure all loose items on deck. Remove all loose equipment from the cockpit area ready to receive the diver/winchman. If the helicopter pilot says he will lower a 'hi-line' to you, have a crew member ready wearing gloves and with a bucket in which to coil the line.

- Put the best helmsman at the wheel, as it is very important to steer a straight course and not veer off.

- Have the crew wear waterproof clothing as the down draught from the helicopter kicks up a good deal of fine spray.

- Have the hand-held radio in the cockpit ready to receive a briefing from the pilot.

HM Coastguard search and rescue helicopter. Photo: Ken Waylen.

10 Rules of the Road

10.1

No. Every vessel is responsible for avoiding collisions but the rules DO describe vessels as being the 'give way' or the 'stand on' vessel. The rules require the 'stand on' vessel to take avoiding action if the other vessel appears to be ignoring a collision situation.

10.2

This flag is used when the vessel has a diver down. Approaching vessels should keep clear of the area and keep a good lookout for divers in the water.

10.3

Spray and cold may deter the crew of a sailing yacht from keeping an adequate lookout to windward. Large foresails will also shield the leeward side when other vessels could approach without being noticed (Figure A10.1).

Fig A10.1 *This headsail is seriously restricting vision to leeward.*

Some modern motor cruisers have poor visibility astern due to superstructure. Care should be taken to post a lookout with a good view aft. At night, it takes approximately 30 minutes to regain full night vision, so care must be taken with torches or cabin lighting when underway at night. Dim objects may go unnoticed during the period of readjustment. Photo-chromic spectacles have been shown to restrict light entering the eye at night, so night watch keepers should keep another plain pair on board.

10.4

A compass bearing of the other vessel should be taken (Fig A10.2). If the bearing does not change, or is very slow to change, then a risk of collision exists. Bearings on large craft should be taken on the same part of the ship on each occasion.

Fig A10.2 *Taking a compass bearing.*

10.5

a) Starboard.

b) The official wording is '... impede the passage of a vessel which can safely navigate only within a narrow channel or fairway.' If your answer has a similar meaning then it may be marked as correct.

10.6

a) One prolonged blast. A prolonged blast should be of four to six seconds duration.

b) One prolonged blast and two short blasts. A short blast is for one second.

c) At intervals not exceeding two minutes.

10.7

a) A sailing vessel underway, port aspect.

b) A power-driven vessel under 50m in length underway, bow aspect.

c) A sailing vessel under 20m in length, underway, bow aspect.

d) A power-driven vessel underway, probably over 50m in length, starboard aspect.

e) A stern light of any vessel, an anchor light of a vessel under 50m in length; a vessel under 7m in length and capable of no more than 7kn, or a street lamp!

f) A power-driven vessel underway, probably over 50m in length, bow aspect.

10.8

a) Both vessels should give way. Each should alter course to starboard and sound one short blast on the horn.

b) B is the give-way vessel as he is overtaking A. Notice that the mode of propulsion does not matter – the overtaking vessel always keeps clear. B should alter course to port to pass astern of A.

c) A is the give-way boat because he is to windward of B. He should bear away and gybe to go astern of B.

d) B is the give-way vessel as he is on port tack. He should bear away to pass astern of A or tack.

e) A is the give-way boat. She should sound one short blast and alter course to starboard to pass behind B.

f) A is the give-way boat. He should either slow down to let B pass ahead or alter course to keep clear.

10.9

a) A black ball should be hoisted in the forward part of the vessel when at anchor during the day.

b) A black cone should be hoisted point down in the forward part of the vessel to indicate that the boat is motor sailing.

10.10

The lights should be changed as the tricolour light is for sailing only. The low port, starboard and stern lights should be switched on together with the 'steaming light', which is mounted higher on the mast. The tricolour light must be turned off. Figure A10.3 shows the configuration for a yacht under 20m.

Fig A10.3 *Yacht with sidelights and steaming light.*

11 Pilotage

11.1

a) The skipper should draw a clearing bearing southward from the eastern side of Burhou to pass to the east of Pierre au Vraic. A bearing of 028°M on the right-hand edge of Burhou is ideal.

b) A bearing of more than 106°M on the Noires Putes will mean that the rock has been passed.

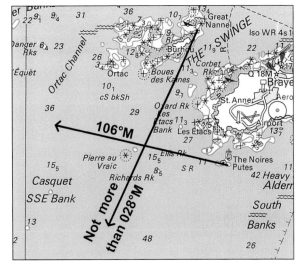

Fig A11.1 *Question 11.1.*

11.2

The boat is approaching in the green sector of the isophase breakwater light. The green light will be on for 2secs and off for 2secs.

11.3

a) The helmsman should alter course to port to get the lights back into line.

b) As soon as the red sector of Sorel Point light becomes visible he can head north until he sees the light turn to white. So long as he remains in the white sector of the light, he will clear the rocks.

11.4

a) He should keep Belvedere House in transit with the white patch on Castle Cornet (223°T) to remain on the leading line.

b) Yes, the boat is under 15m in length and under power so it may enter, provided it keeps well clear of the fairways.

c) Ships and fast ferries.

d) Call St Peter Port Marina on Channel M or 80.

e) Diesel is available at Castle Pier between 0730 and 1730 on weekdays and between 0730 and 1200 on Sunday but the pier is tidal and there is a risk of grounding at some states of the tide.

Safe hours are 3hrs either side of HW so our cruiser must wait a while before picking up fuel.

f) The speed limit is 6kn near the entrance but 4kn closer to the marina.

g) The table in Figure A11.2 shows that there is 1.53m of water over the sill 2½hrs before HW.

    If there is a swell in the harbour it would be prudent to wait another 15mins before entering.

h) Either the harbour master's staff control entry or red and green lights are used.

Ht (m) of HW St Peter Port	Depth of Water in metres over the Sill (dries 4·2 m)						
	HW	±1hr	±2hrs	±2½hrs	±3hrs	±3½hrs	±4hrs
6·20	2·00	1·85	1·55	1·33	1·10	0·88	0·65
·60	2·40	2·18	1·75	1·43	1·10	0·77	0·45
7·00	2·80	2·52	1·95	1·53	1·10	0·67	0·25
·40	3·20	2·85	2·15	1·63	1·10	0·57	0·05
·80	3·60	3·18	2·35	1·73	1·10	0·47	0·00
8·20	4·00	3·52	2·55	1·83	1·10	0·37	0·00
·60	4·40	3·85	2·75	1·93	1·10	0·28	0·00
9·00	4·80	4·18	2·95	2·03	1·10	0·18	0·00
·40	5·20	4·52	3·15	2·13	1·10	0·08	0·00
·80	5·60	4·85	3·35	2·23	1·10	0·00	0·00

Fig A11.2

11.5

a) Use the *Almanac* for port information, tide tables and tidal stream information. Use the pilot book for an aerial picture and port information.

b) The chart is based on the European datum (1950) and the *Almanac* chartlets on WGS 84. If it is possible to change datums on the ship's GNSS then this should be done but if not, the note on the bottom left-hand corner of the chart shows the correction to be made to convert Euro 50 charts to the WGS 84 datum.

c) *Dangers*: Ferries turning.

    Restrictions: Yachts are not allowed in the area adjacent to the Port Militaire.

d) The minimum depth is 2.1m at datum; sufficient for our craft.

e) Pontoons M, N, P and Q are available for visitors.

f) Channel 9.

g) See Figures A11.3 and A11.4.

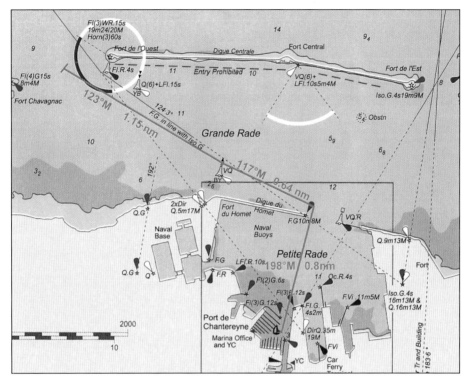

Fig A11.3 *Cherbourg tracks and distances.*

LEAVE TO PORT	LEAVE TO STARBOARD
Fort de l'Ouest (on breakwater)	Fort on Digue Querqueville
Red buoy (Fl R 4s) off rocks	North Cardinal buoy
South Cardinal buoy	Corner of Digue du Homet
Red can buoy (VQ R)	Marina west breakwater wall
Harbour wall (Fl (3) R 12s)	

Fig A11.4 *Cherbourg pilotage.*

12 Aids to Navigation and Passage Planning

12.1

a) True. If the log under-reads, dangers such as rocks or shallow areas may be reached earlier than expected.

b) False. Anti-fouling paint makes the light paddle wheel more difficult to turn; paint on the shaft of the wheel can prevent it turning altogether.

c) True. The paddle wheel will turn as the boat moves through the water, not when the boat is stationary and drifting on the tide.

d) True. A paddle wheel that is covered in barnacles or blocked with weed will turn more slowly so that the log under-reads. Most modern logs have the facility for withdrawing the paddle wheel from the hull and replacing it with a blanking plug when the boat is in harbour.

   It is also advisable to withdraw the log when the boat is being lifted out of the water on slings to prevent accidental damage.

12.2

a) With the depth set below the keel, the boat will run aground when the sounder reads zero so no calculations are necessary to appreciate the amount of remaining water.

b) This can be useful because it shows the true height of tide when over a charted depth.

c) This setting has no advantages except for those who are unable to understand the instruction book on how to change the setting! Going aground when the sounder reads 1.2m in a boat that draws 1.7m is an unnecessary complication!

12.3

i) Low voltage on the ship's batteries.

ii) Lightning strikes giving a power surge in close proximity to the boat.

iii) Damage to the antenna.

iv) Antenna covered so that it cannot receive the signal.

v) Interference from mobile phones.

12.4

a) Access to Hérel marina at Granville is from HW −2½hrs to HW +3½hrs = 1033–1633.

b) Distance = 25½M.

c) Approximately 4hrs 15mins.

d) The stream becomes east-going for Granville at HW St Helier −4½hrs = 0847 BST.

   Stream remains favourable until HW St Helier +30mins = 1347 BST.

e) It is neaps so there is 24hr entry into and exit from Les Bas-Sablons marina.

f) Leaving at 0830 BST should give plenty of time in hand before the stream off Granville becomes west-going.

12.5

a) Granville harbour entrance is rough with a strong westerly wind and as the water is shallow, there may be a big swell on the approach (see Granville Port Information, extract 17). Going on is not a good idea.

   If we turn back to St Malo, we will have to beat to windward against both a rising wind and the tide, so progress could be very slow, wet and demoralising. Seeking shelter would be the best option.

b) There are marked anchorages in the lee of the land just north of Cancale on the western side of the Baie du Mont St-Michel. The nature of the seabed is shown as mud so holding should be good. If the wind veers to the north-west later, the anchorage will remain sheltered.

12.6

a) Approximately 28M.

b) HW Dover 1305 BST. Springs.

c) South or south-east-going stream from HW Dover +2½hrs until HW +6½hrs = 1535 until 1935.

d) Allowing 7.5M covered each hour the passage time would be around 3hrs and 45mins.

e) HW St Helier 2055 BST.

f) Access is from HW −3 to HW +3hrs = 1755–2355. (See St Helier Port Information.)

g) Leave St Peter Port at 1530.

h) *Prominent landmarks:*
    i)   St Martin's Point
    ii) Corbière lighthouse
    iii) Lookout tower close to Point Corbière
    iv) Noirmont Point

   Waypoints:

WP1	0.4M W of SCM Guernsey	49° 25'.9N	002° 29'.1W
WP2	W of overfalls off Corbière	49° 10'.4N	002° 17'.5W
WP3	Off NCM Jersey west passage	49° 09'.9N	002° 12'.2W
WP4	St Helier entrance	49° 10'.0N	002° 07'.2W

   Hazards:
   Ferries and shipping around St Peter Port and St Helier
   Overfalls and off-lying rocks at Point Corbière
   Tide race off Noirmont Point.

13 Weather

13.1
A strong wind warning is issued when winds of force 6 are expected.

13.2
b) B. The wind speed for Beaufort force 8 is 34–40kn.

13.3
a) Sea state moderate = wave height of 1.25–2.5m.

b) Poor visibility = visibility of 1000m to 2M.

c) Soon = expected between 6 and 12hrs from the time of issue of the forecast.

d) Backing = wind altering in an anticlockwise direction, ie NW to SW.

13.4
a) The broadcasts will be announced on VHF Channel 16.

b) ii) As from February 2007, HMCG broadcast weather information three hourly. Times are shown in nautical almanacs.

13.5

a) 3   g) 10

b) 4   h) 8

c) 1   i) 7

d) 2   j) 11

e) 9   k) 5

f) 6

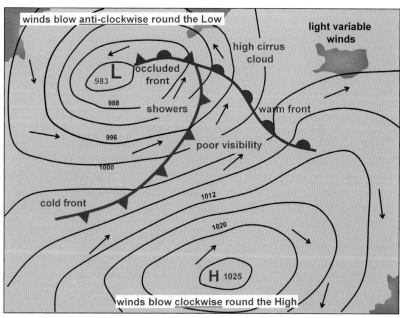

Fig A13.1

13.6

Cloud B will be found in position 10, after the cold front. There could be squally showers from this towering cumulus cloud.

13.7

It would be best to go when the wind and tide are running in the same direction even though this means taking adverse tidal stream. With both together, the sea should be flat and allow full speed to be maintained throughout the passage.

13.8

The anchorage just to the east of Bec du Nez would give the most shelter.

13.9

The increase in wind is caused by 'a sea breeze'. This happens on fine summer days as the land heats up more quickly than the relatively cold sea. The air above the land is heated by the warm sun and rises away from the surface. This leaves slack pressure at ground level that allows air to be drawn in off the sea towards the land. As the land gets even hotter the wind will strengthen and then veer (alter direction clockwise). As the heat from the sun decreases at the end of the day the wind will die away again.

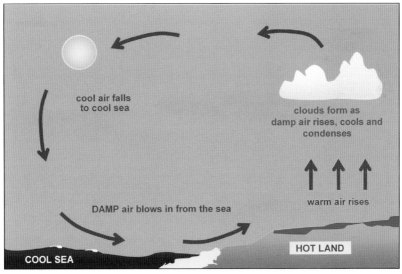

Fig A13.2 *Sea breeze.*

13.10

The wind could strengthen considerably if the cool mountain air rushes down the mountain slope. A quiet overnight anchorage could become very uncomfortable, particularly if the boat is anchored at the entrance to a valley. This type of wind is known as a 'katabatic wind'.

COMMUNICATIONS

14 Communications

14.1

c) 16 miles.

For those who enjoy mathematical formulae, the calculation is:

2.1 × √ antenna height in metres = distance to horizon in nautical miles

ie 2.1 × √16 = 2.1 × 4 = 8.4M for each boat.

This gives a **theoretical** distance of 16.8M as shown in Figure A14.1. High power will have to be used to achieve this theoretical distance.

In practice, two yachts beating to windward in a choppy sea may have the theoretical distance reduced to under 10M.

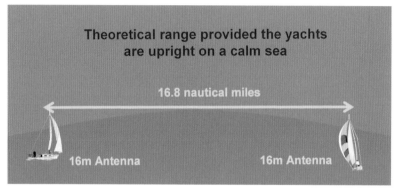

Theoretical range provided the yachts are upright on a calm sea

16.8 nautical miles

16m Antenna   16m Antenna

Fig A14.1

14.2

a) The squelch control limits the annoying background hiss and affects reception only. If it is turned too high some distant transmissions may be lost.

14.3

Channel 16 is the international distress and calling channel and should be kept as free as possible for distress working. When routinely calling another vessel, use DSC if possible as 16 is bypassed with this calling method. If Channel 16 has to be used then do not remain on it for more than one minute.

14.4

a) The red button should be pressed from three to five seconds. Note that most sets require that the button is depressed once before being pressed for three to five seconds.

b) The boat's position, time (UTC), MMSI and type of distress if designated.

c) *Flamingo* has a radio that is licensed in the UK. The numbers 232, 233, 234 and 235 are allocated to the UK, Northern Ireland and other offshore islands.

d) The correct message is given in Figure A14.2.

> Mayday, Mayday, Mayday
> This is *Flamingo*, *Flamingo*, *Flamingo*,
> Callsign ZQM3, MMSI 235899986
> Mayday *Flamingo*, Callsign ZQM3, MMSI 235899986
> In Position 49° 52'.43N 006° 12'.53W
> Serious engine fire
> I require immediate assistance
> We are a motor cruiser with three people on board
> Abandoning to liferaft with a hand-held radio
> Over

Fig A14.2

14.5
a) and c).

14.6
Channel 03. It would be impossible to communicate with another craft using one antenna on this two-frequency (duplex) channel. Duplex frequencies were used for ship-to-shore telephone calls, which are no longer available in the UK. Some of the, now spare, channels are used by HMCG for maritime information broadcasts.

14.7
c) Channel M1.

14.8
To Ofcom, online.

Full instructions for completing this form (Figure A14.3) are given on the Ofcom website www.ofcom.org.uk; the Ship Radio Licence is free provided that that the application is completed online. Any change of ownership or equipment must be reported immediately and the licence should be renewed every 10 years.

14.9

a) Charlie

b) Hotel

c) Mike

d) November

e) Romeo

f) Victor

g) Yankee

14.10

d) Out.

15 The Diesel Engine

15.1

i) C   ii) D   iii) B   iv) A   v) F   vi) E   vii) H   viii) G

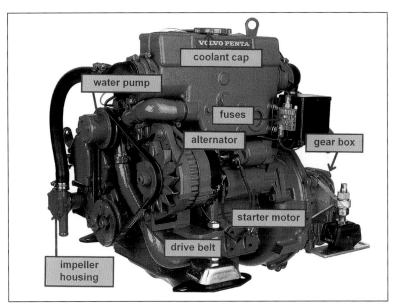

Fig A15.1 *Parts of the diesel engine.*

15.2

a) Suck – fresh air is sucked into each of the cylinders in turn.

b) Squeeze – the air is compressed sufficiently to give it great heat.

c) Bang – misted diesel fuel is injected into the hot air and burns. The burning causes the air to expand, forcing the piston down.

d) Blow – the exhaust valve opens to release the burned gases through the exhaust pipe.

15.3

a) The drive belt should be checked for wear and for correct tensioning. Black powder deposits and worn teeth on the belt show that it is probably slipping and/or worn out.

b) The oil level should be tested using the dipstick. The level should be somewhere between the two graduations on the stick. Avoid over-filling as much as under-filling.

c) The seacock should be closed before the top is removed from the raw water filter so those above waterline installations do not get an air lock and those below the waterline do not flood the boat. Clean seaweed and rubbish from the gauze filter and reassemble, being careful not to cross-thread the top.

d) Remove the coolant cap while the engine is cold. Check that the liquid is at the level recommended by the manufacturer. If topping up is required fill with coolant/corrosion inhibitor if you have it. Otherwise, use fresh, clean water.

15.4
In any order: i) dirt   ii) water   iii) air

15.5
Amateurs should not attempt to dismantle these precision instruments, as they require expert calibration and are very expensive. They should be sent to special service centres for recalibration.

15.6
a) False. Diesel engines need to be warmed up thoroughly and worked under load to give them a long life.

b) True. See answer to a).

c) True. See answer to a).

d) False. All the metal surfaces are unlubricated at start-up and starting at full throttle will cause wear to the moving parts and destroy a turbo.

e) True. Pulling this lever stops delivery of fuel to the injectors.

f) False. Switching the power switch off will not stop the engine but may burn the alternator out in some engines. Unlike petrol engines, most diesels do not require electricity to run, just to turn them over at start-up.

15.7
1) Fuel tank   2) Fuel shut-off valve   3) Pre-filter   4) Fuel lift pump
5) Fine filter   6) Fuel injection pump   7) Injectors

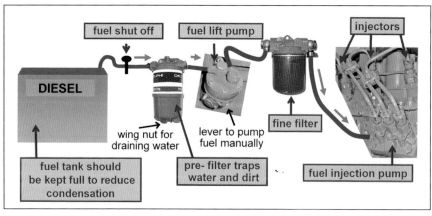

Fig A15.2

16 General

16.1

a) Tide rips, overfalls.

b) Dangerous wreck.

c) Marina.

d) Rock awash at chart datum.

16.2

a) 3.2m (tide) +3.8m (charted depth) = 7.0m.

b) 3.2m (tide) –1.6m (drying height) = 1.6m.

16.3

48° 41'.1N 002° 18'.9W.

16.4

Friday 31 August.

HW Dover 0123 BST Range 6.0m, springs

HW hour 0053–0153 BST

HW +1hr = 0153–0253 251°T 1.3kn.

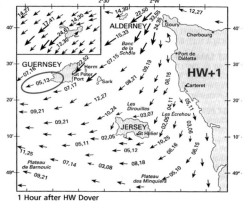

Fig TP1A.1 *Question 16.4.*

16.5

a) Round turn and two half hitches.
   This is a good knot because it can be undone under load and the round turn prevents chafe on the rope.

b) Braided rope.

16.6

a) This wind is more with the tide than against it and this will calm the sea. The land will give shelter inshore.
b) ii) south-westerly.
c) If the wind were in the north-east, the passage would be along a rocky lee shore. Although the wind would be with the tide and the sea reasonably flat, the shore would be unsheltered. The skipper would be advised to sail a few miles off the coast for safety.
   With a south-westerly force 5 wind blowing against the tide the seas will be choppy at best and may be rough where the sea bed is irregular and a strong stream is running. If the crew are inexperienced or prone to sea sickness the skipper may wish to stay in the St Malo area until it moderates.

16.7

a) East cardinal buoy.

b) White light.

c) Quick or very quick flashing 3.

d) Pass to the east of the buoy.

16.8

a) The red button should be pressed from 3–5 seconds.

b) The boat's position, time (UTC), MMSI and type of distress if designated.

c) Mayday, Mayday, Mayday

This is *Hole-in-One, Hole-in-One, Hole-in-One,*

Callsign GB2A, MMSI 235899986

Mayday *Hole-in-One*, Callsign GB2A, MMSI 235899986

In Position 48° 45'.0N 001° 40'.0W

Badly holed and sinking

I require immediate assistance

We are a sailing yacht with three people on board

Preparing to abandon to liferaft

Over

16.9

Picture A In this picture, B is the give-way vessel as he is on port tack. He should ease sheets and bear away to pass behind A or tack to parallel his course.

Picture B Two power-driven vessels are crossing so A is the give-way vessel (he can see the port side and red light of B). He should sound one short blast on his horn and alter course to starboard.

Picture C Boat A has to give way, as he is the windward boat. He should bear away to pass behind B or slow down to let B pass ahead.

16.10

a) A power-driven vessel of less than 50m in length, bow aspect.

b) A sailing vessel, port aspect, any length.

c) A power-driven vessel, probably over 50m in length, starboard aspect.

16.11

a) One prolonged blast (4–6secs) at intervals not exceeding 2mins.

b) One prolonged and two short blasts at intervals not exceeding 2mins.

16.12

A black ball towards the bow where it can best be seen.

17 General

17.1

a) A sheet bend.

b) For joining ropes of unequal diameters, ie when rafting up alongside in a crowded harbour it is sometimes necessary to join two ropes to lengthen the shorelines.

17.2

a) Pre-stretched polyester or, for performance craft where weight is a factor, the more advanced, exotic (and more expensive) Dyneema, Kevlar, Technora, or Vectren.

b) Polypropylene. This type of rope floats and will remain on the surface ready for the casualty to grab.

c) Nylon, as it stretches and has high tensile strength.

17.3

a) A drying wreck that has superstructure visible at chart datum.

b) Windmill.

c) A major light. The magenta tear-drop indicates that it is lit and the small hole in the centre of the star indicates that it is a major light.

d) A rock that covers and uncovers with the tide.

17.4

49° 43'.4N 002° 22'.5W.

17.5

a) 4.3m (tide) −2.3 (drying height) = 2.0m.

b) 4.3m (tide) +2.8 (charted depth) = 7.1m.

17.6

a) South cardinal mark.

b) White.

c) The triangular top marks on cardinal buoys point to the position of the black paint. In figure TP2.3 the triangles are pointing downwards, to the bottom of the buoy and to the bottom of the chart, ie the south. If either the paint or the top mark is missing, we will still know that it is a south cardinal mark.

d) Alter course to port to leave the buoy on your starboard side.

17.7

i) Do not overload the dinghy; load it evenly.

ii) The crew should wear lifejackets.

iii) Take the pump, bailer and hand-held radio with you.

iv) Carry oars if you are using an outboard motor.

v) Carry a torch at night.

17.8

Picture A Both A and B alter course. Vessels that are head on, or nearly head on, are required to sound one short blast on the horn and alter course to starboard.

Picture B Red yacht B is overtaking the smaller motor boat and must give way.

Picture C Powerboat A should give way to the vessel under sail. It would be most helpful if he altered course to port to pass down the lee side of the yacht but care should always be taken when turning towards a vessel that you are attempting to avoid.

17.9

a) This could be an anchor light, the stern light of a vessel underway, a man in a rowing boat holding a torch or even a street lamp.

b) A sailing vessel, starboard aspect. The length is indefinite as it may be a tri-lantern of a boat under 20m or the bow light of a large and high sail training vessel.

c) Power-driven vessel probably over 50m in length, bow aspect.

17.10

Take bearings with the hand-bearing compass. If the bearings do not appreciably change then a risk of collision exists.

17.11

a) A strong wind warning is issued when the wind is expected to reach force 6.

b) A gale warning is issued when the wind is expected to reach force 8 (more than 34kn) or gust to 43kn.

17.12

i) Dress in warm clothes and wear lifejackets.

ii) Leave the saloon quickly, taking a fire extinguisher with you. Try not to inhale the toxic fumes.

iii) Collect the flare box and hand-held radio. If there's time, grab some food and water and/or the grab bag.

iv) Prepare to launch the liferaft from the windward side of the boat.

v) Tie the liferaft painter to the boat.

vi) Try to stay dry if possible.

vii) Once in the liferaft, cut the painter and paddle away from the boat.

viii) Take seasickness pills and BELIEVE that you will be rescued.

This crew member is taking no chances dressed in foul weather gear, safety harness and life jacket.

18 Chartwork

18.1

See plot in Figure TPA3.1 (see page 98). Position 48° 43'.5N 001° 56'.8W.

18.2

See plot in Figure TPA3.1 (see page 98).

a) Wednesday 15 August. HW St Helier 2106 BST. Range 9.2m, springs

HW hour 2036–2136. Time at buoy 1736 = HW hr −3

Ⓡ HW − 3hrs 1736–1836 = 102°T 2.3kn ½hr = 1.15M

Magnetic course to steer = 176°T 179°M.

b) Just under half an hour.

c) Speed over ground = 24.7kn.

d) The helmsman will have to add 10° to his course to remain on the desired track. Course to steer 189°M (practically 190°M).

18.3

See plot in Figure TPA3.1 (see page 98).

a) Position at 1135 48° 46'.0N 002° 02'.3W.

b) Saturday 16 June. HW St Helier 0805 BST. Range 8.7m. Use spring rate

HW hour 0735–0835. Required time 1135

Ⓡ 1135–1235 = HW +4hrs = 276°T 1.6kn

No, if the yacht continues on the same course it will probably hit the lighthouse!

c) Course over ground = 197°T.

18.4

Saturday 9 June. St Helier

HW 1334 BST 8.7m LW 2007 3.3m Range 5.4m (nearly neaps)

a) Height of tide at 1704. BST = 5.7m. See Figure TPA3.2

b) Fall to LW = 5.7m −3.3m = 2.4m

c) Depth of water less fall less draught = clearance

5.0m −2.4m −2.0m = 0.6m.

Continued on page 98

The skipper wished to have a 1.5m clearance but will only have 0.6m of water under the keel at LW. We must never forget that the tide tables are a prediction and the height of tide will alter with changing weather conditions. A clearance of half a metre is not a safe amount so the skipper should move the boat into deeper water.

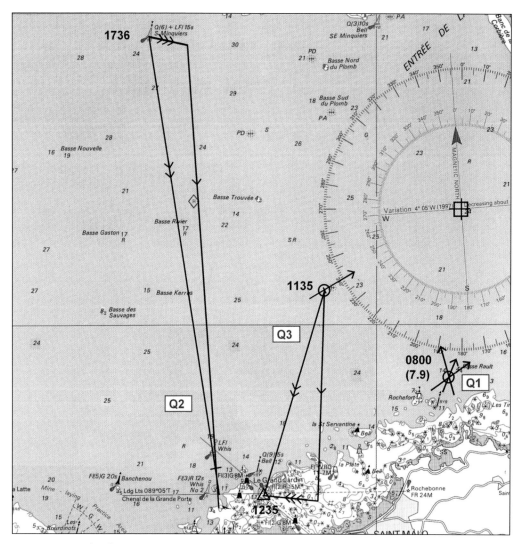

Fig TPA3.1 *Plot for questions 18.1, 2 and 3.*

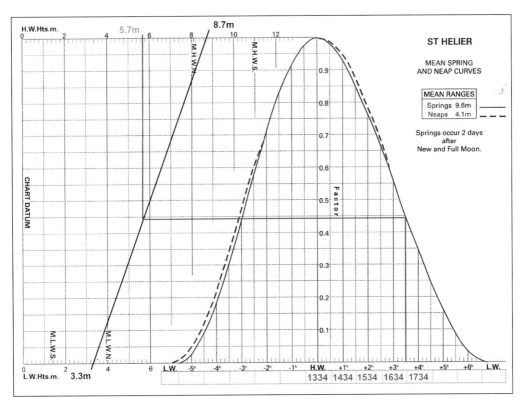

Fig TPA3.2 *Question 18.4.*

19 Chartwork

19.1
See plot in Figure TPA4.1. 49° 26'.3N 002° 30'.1W.

19.2
See plot in Figure TPA4.1

a) Monday 23 July:

HW St Helier 1259 BST. Range 4.1m, neaps

HW hour = 1229–1329

Time leaving the buoy = 1130 so use:

⬦F   HW –1hr = 1129–1239 039°T 2.1kn

Course to steer 117°T +3°W = 120°M. See plot in Figure TP4.1.

b) SOG = 5.8kn.

c) ETA = about 35–40mins.

d) The alteration of course should be towards the wind so 5° should be subtracted. Course to steer now 115°M.

19.3
a) See plot in Figure TPA4.1.

b) The course over the ground passes to the south of the tide rips.

c) The COG is 259°T.

19.4
Thursday 17 May:

HW St Helier 1950 11.2m LW (18 May) 0236 1.0m. Range 10.2m, springs (mean spring range = 9.6m)

Time of anchoring = 2150 = HW +2hrs

a) Height of tide at 2150 = 8.7m

b)
Height of tide	8.7m
Height of LW	1.0m –
Fall to LW	7.7m

c) Depth of water in which to anchor = Fall 7.7m + draught 1.2m + clearance 2.0m

Answer 10.9m.

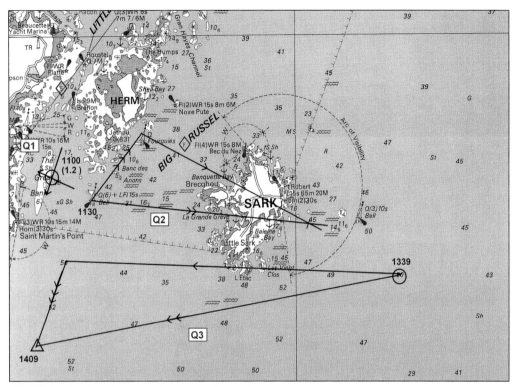

Fig TPA4.1 *Plots for questions 19.1, 2 and 3.*

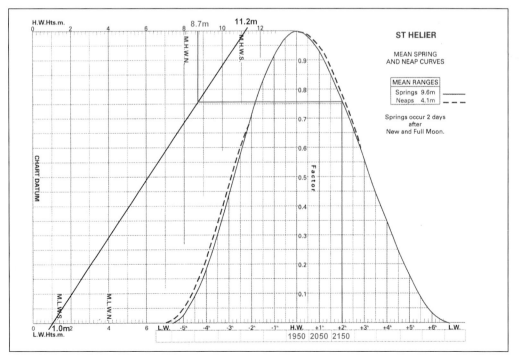

Fig TPA4.2 *Question 19.4.*

EXTRACT 1: DOVER TIDE TABLES

Extract 1: Dover Tide Tables

TIME ZONE (UT)	DOVER LAT 51°07'N LONG 1°19'E	Dates in red are SPRINGS
For Summer Time add ONE hour in non-shaded areas	TIMES AND HEIGHTS OF HIGH AND LOW WATERS	Dates in blue are NEAPS

YEAR **2007**

MAY

Day	Time m	Time m	Day	Time m	Time m
1	0540 1.2 / 1042 6.1	TU 1756 1.3 / 2256 6.3	16	0524 0.8 / 1021 6.6	W 1745 0.8 / ●2240 6.8
2	0609 1.2 / 1112 6.2	W 1823 1.2 / ○2325 6.3	17	0618 0.7 / 1105 6.7	TH 1834 0.8 / 2326 6.8
3	0636 1.2 / 1141 6.2	TH 1850 1.2 / 2351 6.2	18	0705 0.7 / 1150 6.7	F 1920 0.8
4	0705 1.2 / 1206 6.2	F 1919 1.2	19	0012 6.7 / 0749 0.8	SA 1236 6.6 / 2004 0.9
5	0013 6.2 / 0735 1.2	SA 1229 6.2 / 1950 1.4	20	0059 6.6 / 0831 1.1	SU 1323 6.5 / 2049 1.1
6	0039 6.2 / 0806 1.3	SU 1257 6.2 / 2023 1.4	21	0148 6.3 / 0914 1.4	M 1413 6.2 / 2135 1.4
7	0111 6.1 / 0840 1.5	M 1333 6.1 / 2059 1.6	22	0240 5.9 / 1001 1.7	TU 1505 6.0 / 2227 1.6
8	0152 5.9 / 0918 1.7	TU 1420 5.8 / 2142 1.8	23	0337 5.6 / 1054 2.0	W 1600 5.7 / ◐2326 1.9
9	0246 5.6 / 1005 1.9	W 1524 5.6 / 2238 2.0	24	0439 5.3 / 1156 2.2	TH 1702 5.5
10	0412 5.4 / 1108 2.1	TH 1654 5.4 / ◑2357 2.0	25	0030 2.0 / 0552 5.2	F 1300 2.2 / 1812 5.4
11	0551 5.4 / 1241 2.1	F 1815 5.5	26	0132 1.9 / 0708 5.3	SA 1401 2.1 / 1923 5.5
12	0122 1.8 / 0701 5.6	SA 1358 1.8 / 1921 5.8	27	0229 1.8 / 0805 5.4	SU 1458 2.0 / 2020 5.7
13	0229 1.5 / 0759 5.9	SU 1459 1.5 / 2017 6.2	28	0321 1.7 / 0851 5.6	M 1549 1.8 / 2106 5.8
14	0328 1.2 / 0850 6.2	M 1555 1.3 / 2107 6.5	29	0408 1.5 / 0930 5.8	TU 1634 1.6 / 2145 6.0
15	0426 0.9 / 0937 6.4	TU 1651 1.0 / 2154 6.7	30	0450 1.4 / 1006 6.0	W 1714 1.5 / 2221 6.0
			31	0528 1.3 / 1041 6.1	TH 1750 1.4 / 2254 6.1

JUNE

Day	Time m	Time m	Day	Time m	Time m
1	0606 1.3 / 1114 6.2	F 1825 1.3 / ○2326 6.1	16	0653 1.0 / 1143 6.5	SA 1910 1.0
2	0642 1.3 / 1146 6.2	SA 1902 1.3 / 2358 6.1	17	0007 6.5 / 0740 1.1	SU 1228 6.5 / 1958 1.0
3	0719 1.3 / 1219 6.2	SU 1939 1.3	18	0054 6.4 / 0825 1.2	M 1313 6.5 / 2044 1.1
4	0032 6.1 / 0755 1.3	M 1254 6.2 / 2016 1.3	19	0139 6.2 / 0907 1.3	TU 1358 6.4 / 2128 1.2
5	0110 6.1 / 0833 1.4	TU 1335 6.2 / 2057 1.4	20	0224 6.0 / 0948 1.5	W 1443 6.2 / 2211 1.4
6	0155 6.0 / 0914 1.5	W 1423 6.1 / 2142 1.5	21	0311 5.8 / 1027 1.7	TH 1529 6.0 / 2253 1.6
7	0248 5.8 / 1001 1.7	TH 1519 6.0 / 2234 1.6	22	0401 5.6 / 1108 1.9	F 1618 5.8 / ◐2338 1.8
8	0352 5.7 / 1056 1.8	F 1621 5.9 / ◑2337 1.6	23	0456 5.4 / 1154 2.1	SA 1713 5.6
9	0505 5.7 / 1203 1.8	SA 1729 5.9	24	0027 1.9 / 0557 5.2	SU 1250 2.2 / 1813 5.4
10	0044 1.6 / 0616 5.7	SU 1313 1.8 / 1836 5.9	25	0123 2.0 / 0700 5.3	M 1352 2.2 / 1917 5.4
11	0149 1.5 / 0721 5.8	M 1418 1.6 / 1940 6.1	26	0220 2.0 / 0758 5.4	TU 1453 2.1 / 2015 5.5
12	0251 1.4 / 0819 6.0	TU 1521 1.5 / 2039 6.2	27	0316 1.8 / 0849 5.5	W 1549 1.9 / 2105 5.7
13	0355 1.2 / 0914 6.1	W 1623 1.3 / 2135 6.4	28	0409 1.7 / 0934 5.8	TH 1638 1.7 / 2149 5.8
14	0500 1.1 / 1006 6.3	TH 1724 1.1 / 2229 6.5	29	0457 1.5 / 1015 5.9	F 1723 1.5 / 2230 6.0
15	0600 1.0 / 1056 6.4	F 1819 1.0 / ●2319 6.5	30	0542 1.4 / 1054 6.1	SA 1806 1.3 / ○2309 6.1

JULY

Day	Time m	Time m	Day	Time m	Time m
1	0626 1.3 / 1131 6.2	SU 1848 1.2 / 2347 6.2	16	0005 6.4 / 0735 1.1	M 1219 6.6 / 1952 0.9
2	0708 1.3 / 1208 6.3	M 1931 1.2	17	0045 6.3 / 0815 1.2	TU 1258 6.6 / 2033 1.0
3	0026 6.2 / 0750 1.2	TU 1247 6.4 / 2013 1.1	18	0123 6.3 / 0851 1.2	W 1337 6.5 / 2109 1.1
4	0106 6.2 / 0831 1.2	W 1328 6.5 / 2056 1.1	19	0200 6.1 / 0921 1.4	TH 1415 6.4 / 2140 1.2
5	0147 6.2 / 0911 1.3	TH 1411 6.5 / 2138 1.1	20	0237 6.0 / 0947 1.5	F 1453 6.2 / 2209 1.4
6	0233 6.2 / 0952 1.3	F 1459 6.4 / 2222 1.2	21	0316 5.8 / 1012 1.7	SA 1530 6.0 / 2238 1.6
7	0324 6.0 / 1037 1.4	SA 1551 6.3 / ◑2311 1.3	22	0359 5.5 / 1045 1.9	SU 1613 5.7 / ◐2317 1.9
8	0422 5.9 / 1129 1.6	SU 1650 6.1	23	0452 5.3 / 1130 2.2	M 1709 5.4
9	0007 1.5 / 0529 5.7	M 1231 1.8 / 1757 5.9	24	0010 2.1 / 0559 5.1	TU 1236 2.4 / 1818 5.2
10	0112 1.7 / 0645 5.6	TU 1341 1.9 / 1911 5.8	25	0124 2.2 / 0710 5.1	W 1401 2.4 / 1929 5.3
11	0221 1.7 / 0758 5.6	W 1453 1.8 / 2024 5.9	26	0237 2.2 / 0814 5.3	TH 1512 2.2 / 2033 5.4
12	0333 1.6 / 0904 5.8	TH 1605 1.6 / 2132 6.0	27	0339 1.9 / 0908 5.6	F 1610 1.8 / 2126 5.7
13	0449 1.5 / 1003 6.0	F 1714 1.4 / 2232 6.2	28	0434 1.7 / 0954 5.9	SA 1701 1.5 / 2211 6.0
14	0555 1.3 / 1053 6.3	SA 1814 1.2 / ●2322 6.3	29	0523 1.4 / 1034 6.2	SU 1748 1.3 / 2252 6.2
15	0649 1.2 / 1137 6.5	SU 1906 1.0	30	0610 1.3 / 1112 6.4	M 1835 1.1 / ○2331 6.4
			31	0656 1.1 / 1151 6.6	TU 1920 1.0

AUGUST

Day	Time m	Time m	Day	Time m	Time m
1	0010 6.5 / 0739 1.1	W 1230 6.7 / 2003 0.8	16	0058 6.4 / 0822 1.2	TH 1312 6.6 / 2038 1.0
2	0048 6.5 / 0819 1.0	TH 1309 6.8 / 2044 0.8	17	0129 6.3 / 0843 1.3	F 1343 6.5 / 2100 1.2
3	0127 6.5 / 0856 1.0	F 1350 6.8 / 2122 0.8	18	0158 6.1 / 0902 1.4	SA 1411 6.3 / 2121 1.3
4	0209 6.5 / 0933 1.1	SA 1434 6.7 / 2200 1.0	19	0224 5.9 / 0926 1.5	SU 1437 6.1 / 2147 1.6
5	0255 6.3 / 1012 1.3	SU 1522 6.4 / ◑2242 1.3	20	0250 5.7 / 0957 1.8	M 1508 5.8 / ◐2221 1.9
6	0349 6.0 / 1058 1.6	M 1619 6.1 / 2334 1.7	21	0326 5.4 / 1036 2.1	TU 1556 5.4 / 2306 2.2
7	0456 5.6 / 1157 1.9	TU 1729 5.7	22	0440 5.1 / 1129 2.5	W 1729 5.1
8	0041 2.0 / 0621 5.4	W 1315 2.2 / 1856 5.5	23	0019 2.5 / 0630 5.0	TH 1310 2.6 / 1857 5.1
9	0202 2.1 / 0749 5.4	TH 1439 2.1 / 2027 5.6	24	0203 2.5 / 0743 5.2	F 1442 2.4 / 2008 5.3
10	0331 2.0 / 0905 5.6	F 1605 1.8 / 2141 5.8	25	0315 2.1 / 0843 5.5	SA 1545 1.9 / 2105 5.7
11	0456 1.7 / 1004 6.0	SA 1717 1.4 / 2236 6.1	26	0412 1.7 / 0930 6.0	SU 1638 1.5 / 2151 6.1
12	0555 1.4 / 1048 6.3	SU 1812 1.1 / ●2318 6.3	27	0503 1.4 / 1010 6.3	M 1728 1.2 / 2231 6.4
13	0642 1.2 / 1126 6.5	M 1859 0.9 / 2354 6.4	28	0551 1.2 / 1049 6.6	TU 1816 0.9 / ○2309 6.6
14	0722 1.1 / 1202 6.7	TU 1938 0.9	29	0636 1.0 / 1127 6.9	W 1902 0.7 / 2346 6.8
15	0026 6.4 / 0755 1.1	W 1238 6.7 / 2011 0.9	30	0719 0.9 / 1205 7.0	TH 1944 0.6
			31	0023 6.8 / 0756 0.8	F 1245 7.1 / 2022 0.6

Extract 2A: Tidal Stream Atlas

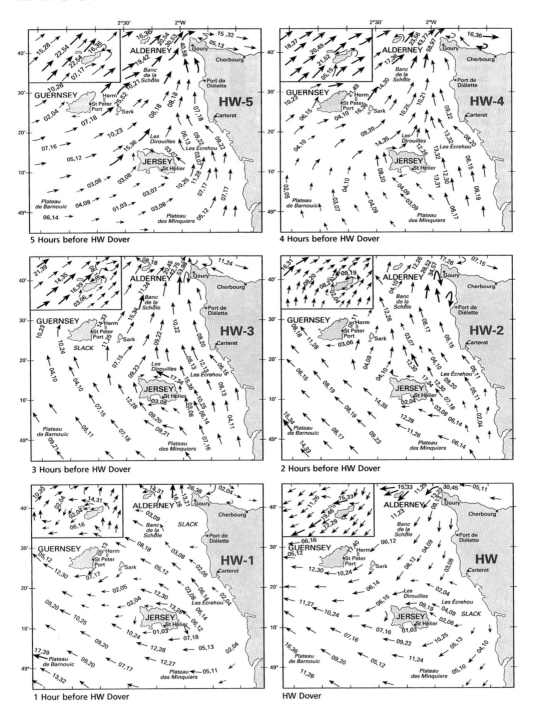

5 Hours before HW Dover

4 Hours before HW Dover

3 Hours before HW Dover

2 Hours before HW Dover

1 Hour before HW Dover

HW Dover

Extract 2B: Tidal Stream Atlas

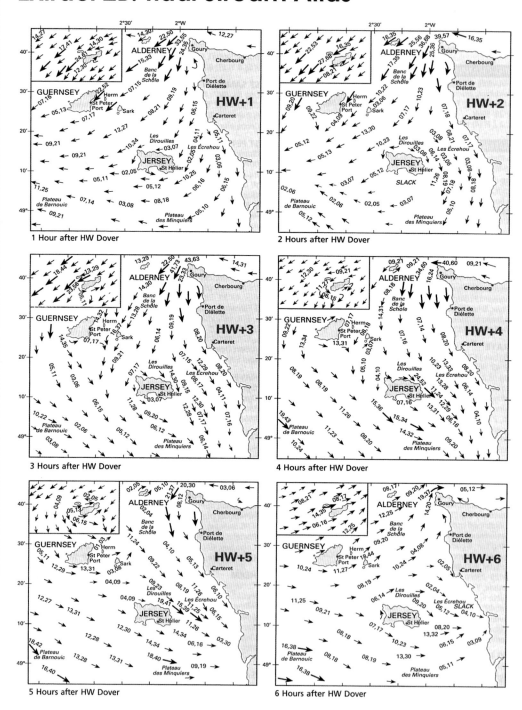

1 Hour after HW Dover

2 Hours after HW Dover

3 Hours after HW Dover

4 Hours after HW Dover

5 Hours after HW Dover

6 Hours after HW Dover

EXTRACTS

Extract 3: St Helier Tide Tables

TIME ZONE (UT) For Summer Time add ONE hour in **non-shaded areas**	**ST HELIER** LAT 49°11'N LONG 2°07'W TIMES AND HEIGHTS OF HIGH AND LOW WATERS	Dates in red are SPRINGS Dates in blue are NEAPS YEAR 2007

MAY

Time m	Time m
1 0006 2.1 / 0547 10.0 / TU 1225 2.0 / 1806 10.1	**16** 0542 10.9 / 1221 1.2 / W 1805 11.0 ●
2 0040 1.9 / 0619 10.1 / W 1257 1.9 / ○ 1837 10.2	**17** 0047 1.1 / 0630 11.1 / TH 1310 1.1 / 1850 11.2
3 0112 1.8 / 0650 10.2 / TH 1328 1.9 / 1906 10.3	**18** 0136 1.0 / 0717 11.0 / F 1356 1.2 / 1933 11.1
4 0144 1.8 / 0720 10.1 / F 1358 2.0 / 1934 10.2	**19** 0221 1.2 / 0802 10.7 / SA 1439 1.6 / 2016 10.7
5 0214 1.9 / 0750 9.9 / SA 1427 2.2 / 2002 10.0	**20** 0306 1.6 / 0846 10.2 / SU 1521 2.1 / 2058 10.2
6 0245 2.2 / 0820 9.7 / SU 1456 2.6 / 2032 9.7	**21** 0349 2.1 / 0931 9.5 / M 1603 2.8 / 2141 9.5
7 0317 2.6 / 0853 9.3 / M 1527 3.0 / 2105 9.3	**22** 0434 2.8 / 1018 8.8 / TU 1648 3.4 / 2229 8.8
8 0353 3.0 / 0932 8.8 / TU 1606 3.4 / 2149 8.8	**23** 0524 3.4 / 1112 8.3 / W 1741 3.9 / ◑ 2327 8.3
9 0439 3.4 / 1025 8.3 / W 1659 3.8 / 2251 8.4	**24** 0623 3.8 / 1218 7.9 / TH 1847 4.1
10 0543 3.6 / 1141 8.0 / TH 1813 4.0 ◐	**25** 0039 8.1 / 0730 3.9 / F 1329 8.0 / 1958 4.1
11 0018 8.2 / 0703 3.6 / F 1310 8.2 / 1941 3.8	**26** 0151 8.1 / 0836 3.7 / SA 1433 8.2 / 2102 3.8
12 0146 8.6 / 0824 3.2 / SA 1429 8.7 / 2100 3.2	**27** 0253 8.4 / 0932 3.4 / SU 1527 8.6 / 2155 3.4
13 0258 9.2 / 0934 2.5 / SU 1532 9.4 / 2205 2.4	**28** 0345 8.7 / 1021 3.1 / M 1613 9.0 / 2242 3.0
14 0358 9.9 / 1035 1.9 / M 1627 10.1 / 2303 1.9	**29** 0429 9.1 / 1104 2.8 / TU 1653 9.4 / 2325 2.7
15 0452 10.5 / 1130 1.4 / TU 1717 10.7 / 2356 1.4	**30** 0510 9.4 / 1145 2.5 / W 1731 9.7
	31 0005 2.4 / 0547 9.6 / TH 1224 2.4 / 1806 9.9

JUNE

Time m	Time m
1 0044 2.2 / 0624 9.7 / F 1301 2.3 / ○ 1840 10.0	**16** 0123 1.5 / 0705 10.4 / SA 1342 1.7 / 1921 10.7
2 0122 2.1 / 0700 9.8 / SA 1337 2.3 / 1915 10.1	**17** 0212 1.5 / 0753 10.3 / SU 1429 1.8 / 2006 10.5
3 0158 2.1 / 0736 9.8 / SU 1412 2.3 / 1950 10.0	**18** 0258 1.7 / 0837 10.1 / M 1512 2.1 / 2048 10.2
4 0234 2.2 / 0814 9.7 / M 1447 2.5 / 2028 9.9	**19** 0341 2.0 / 0919 9.8 / TU 1552 2.5 / 2128 9.8
5 0312 2.3 / 0854 9.5 / TU 1525 2.7 / 2110 9.7	**20** 0421 2.4 / 0959 9.2 / W 1631 2.9 / 2208 9.3
6 0353 2.5 / 0939 9.2 / W 1608 2.9 / 2157 9.4	**21** 0459 2.9 / 1040 8.8 / TH 1709 3.3 / 2250 8.9
7 0440 2.7 / 1029 9.0 / TH 1659 3.2 / 2251 9.1	**22** 0538 3.3 / 1124 8.4 / F 1752 3.7 / ◑ 2339 8.4
8 0535 2.9 / 1128 8.8 / F 1759 3.3 / ◑ 2355 8.9	**23** 0622 3.6 / 1217 8.2 / SA 1844 3.9
9 0637 3.0 / 1234 8.7 / SA 1907 3.3	**24** 0037 8.1 / 0716 3.8 / SU 1320 8.0 / 1945 4.0
10 0105 8.9 / 0745 3.0 / SU 1344 8.9 / 2019 3.1	**25** 0143 8.0 / 0819 3.9 / M 1424 8.1 / 2051 3.9
11 0216 9.1 / 0854 2.7 / M 1452 9.2 / 2128 2.8	**26** 0247 8.1 / 0922 3.7 / TU 1523 8.4 / 2152 3.6
12 0322 9.4 / 0959 2.4 / TU 1554 9.6 / 2232 2.4	**27** 0345 8.4 / 1019 3.4 / W 1614 8.8 / 2246 3.2
13 0424 9.8 / 1101 2.1 / W 1651 10.1 / 2332 2.0	**28** 0436 8.8 / 1110 3.1 / TH 1659 9.2 / 2335 2.8
14 0521 10.1 / 1158 1.9 / TH 1744 10.4	**29** 0522 9.1 / 1157 2.8 / F 1742 9.6
15 0029 1.7 / 0615 10.4 / F 1253 1.7 / ● 1834 10.6	**30** 0021 2.4 / 0605 9.5 / SA 1242 2.5 / ○ 1823 9.9

JULY

Time m	Time m
1 0106 2.1 / 0647 9.7 / SU 1324 2.3 / 1904 10.1	**16** 0205 1.5 / 0742 10.3 / M 1419 1.8 / 1953 10.6
2 0148 1.9 / 0728 9.9 / M 1404 2.1 / 1945 10.3	**17** 0246 1.6 / 0821 10.3 / TU 1457 1.9 / 2031 10.5
3 0229 1.8 / 0810 10.1 / TU 1443 2.1 / 2026 10.4	**18** 0323 1.7 / 0857 10.1 / W 1531 2.1 / 2106 10.2
4 0309 1.8 / 0852 10.1 / W 1524 2.1 / 2108 10.4	**19** 0354 2.0 / 0929 9.8 / TH 1602 2.4 / 2138 9.8
5 0351 1.8 / 0934 10.0 / TH 1606 2.2 / 2151 10.2	**20** 0423 2.4 / 1001 9.4 / F 1631 2.8 / 2210 9.4
6 0433 2.0 / 1018 9.7 / F 1650 2.4 / 2237 9.8	**21** 0450 2.9 / 1033 8.9 / SA 1702 3.3 / 2244 8.8
7 0519 2.3 / 1105 9.4 / SA 1738 2.8 / ◑ 2327 9.4	**22** 0522 3.4 / 1110 8.4 / SU 1740 3.7 / ◑ 2325 8.3
8 0609 2.7 / 1157 9.0 / SU 1834 3.1	**23** 0602 3.9 / 1159 8.0 / M 1831 4.1
9 0026 9.0 / 0707 3.0 / M 1302 8.8 / 1941 3.3	**24** 0022 7.8 / 0700 4.2 / TU 1310 7.7 / 1942 4.3
10 0137 8.8 / 0817 3.2 / TU 1415 8.8 / 2057 3.3	**25** 0142 7.6 / 0819 4.3 / W 1432 7.8 / 2104 4.2
11 0255 8.8 / 0933 3.2 / W 1529 9.0 / 2213 3.0	**26** 0305 7.8 / 0939 4.1 / TH 1541 8.3 / 2214 3.7
12 0410 9.1 / 1044 2.9 / TH 1637 9.5 / 2322 2.5	**27** 0410 8.3 / 1043 3.5 / F 1637 8.8 / 2312 3.1
13 0515 9.5 / 1148 2.5 / F 1735 9.9	**28** 0504 8.9 / 1137 3.0 / SA 1725 9.5
14 0023 2.1 / 0610 9.9 / SA 1245 2.1 / ● 1826 10.3	**29** 0004 2.5 / 0551 9.5 / SU 1226 2.4 / 1809 10.0
15 0118 1.7 / 0658 10.2 / SU 1335 1.9 / 1912 10.6	**30** 0052 2.0 / 0635 10.0 / M 1312 2.0 / ○ 1852 10.5
	31 0138 1.5 / 0717 10.4 / TU 1355 1.6 / 1934 10.9

AUGUST

Time m	Time m
1 0220 1.2 / 0758 10.7 / W 1435 1.4 / 2015 11.1	**16** 0254 1.5 / 0827 10.4 / TH 1501 1.8 / 2036 10.6
2 0300 1.1 / 0838 10.8 / TH 1515 1.4 / 2055 11.1	**17** 0319 1.8 / 0855 10.2 / F 1527 2.1 / 2103 10.2
3 0339 1.1 / 0917 10.7 / F 1553 1.5 / 2135 10.8	**18** 0343 2.2 / 0921 9.8 / SA 1551 2.5 / 2129 9.7
4 0417 1.5 / 0956 10.3 / SA 1633 1.9 / 2215 10.3	**19** 0406 2.7 / 0946 9.3 / SU 1618 3.0 / 2155 9.1
5 0456 2.0 / 1037 9.8 / SU 1714 2.5 / ◑ 2258 9.6	**20** 0431 3.2 / 1013 8.7 / M 1648 3.6 / ◑ 2225 8.4
6 0539 2.7 / 1123 9.1 / M 1803 3.2 / 2352 8.8	**21** 0502 3.9 / 1047 8.1 / TU 1731 4.2 / 2308 7.8
7 0633 3.4 / 1223 8.5 / TU 1911 3.7	**22** 0551 4.5 / 1144 7.6 / W 1840 4.6
8 0107 8.2 / 0750 3.9 / W 1350 8.2 / 2041 3.8	**23** 0029 7.3 / 0717 4.8 / TH 1338 7.4 / 2019 4.6
9 0247 8.1 / 0922 3.8 / TH 1524 8.5 / 2212 3.4	**24** 0232 7.4 / 0904 4.5 / F 1516 7.9 / 2147 4.0
10 0413 8.6 / 1044 3.3 / F 1636 9.1 / 2324 2.7	**25** 0351 8.1 / 1021 3.8 / SA 1617 8.7 / 2251 3.1
11 0515 9.3 / 1147 2.6 / SA 1731 9.8	**26** 0446 8.9 / 1117 3.0 / SU 1706 9.6 / 2344 2.3
12 0020 2.1 / 0603 9.9 / SU 1238 2.1 / ● 1817 10.4	**27** 0533 9.8 / 1207 2.2 / M 1751 10.4
13 0108 1.7 / 0645 10.3 / M 1322 1.7 / 1857 10.7	**28** 0033 1.6 / 0616 10.5 / TU 1254 1.6 / ○ 1834 11.0
14 0149 1.4 / 0723 10.5 / TU 1400 1.6 / 1933 10.8	**29** 0119 1.1 / 0657 11.0 / W 1337 1.2 / 1915 11.5
15 0224 1.4 / 0756 10.5 / W 1433 1.6 / 2006 10.8	**30** 0202 0.7 / 0738 11.3 / TH 1418 0.9 / 1955 11.7
	31 0241 0.6 / 0816 11.4 / F 1457 0.9 / 2034 11.6

HAT is 12.2 metres above Chart Datum

Extract 4: St Helier Tidal Curve

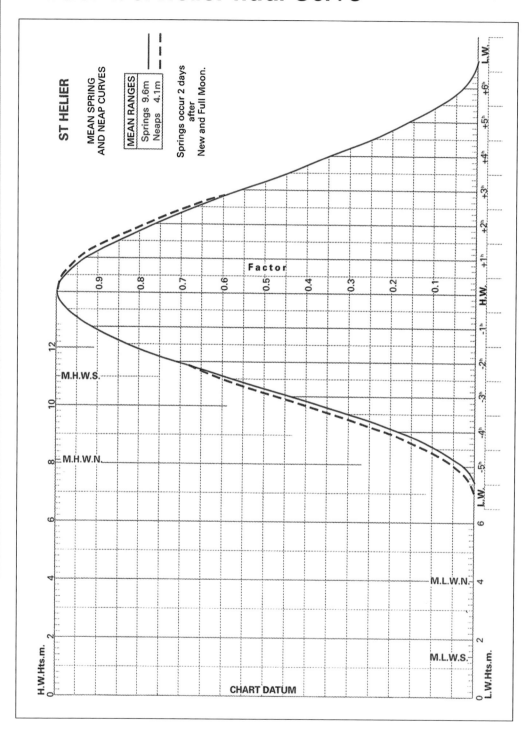

Extract 5: St Helier Approaches Chart

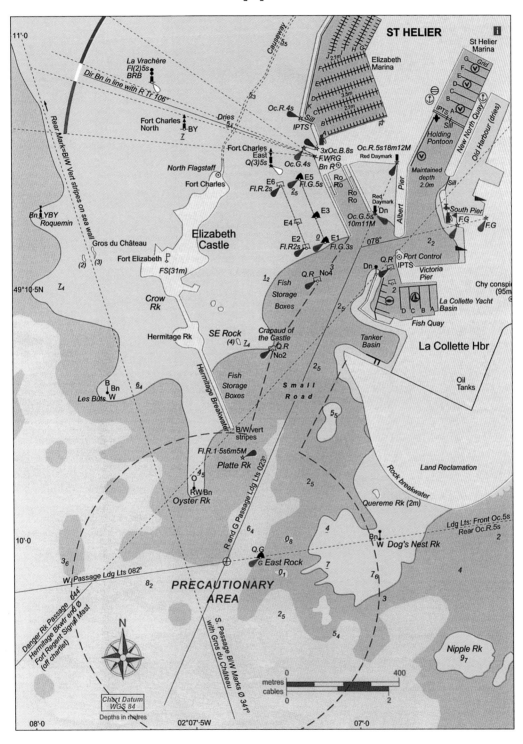

Extract 6: St Helier Port Information

ST HELIER

Jersey 49°10'·57N 02°06'·98W ✵✵✵☆☆

CHARTS AC *3655, 1137*, 3278, *5604*; SHOM 7160, 7161, 6938; Navi 534, 1014; Imray C33B; Stanfords 2, 16, 26

TIDES –0455 Dover; ML 6·1; Duration 0545; Zone 0 (UT) St Helier is a Standard Port (➜). The tidal range is very large.

SHELTER Excellent in 2 marinas, La Collette and adjacent areas.

NAVIGATION WPT (where all appr's converge) 49°09'·95N 02°07'·38W, 023°/0·74M to front 023° ldg lt. WPT is near the centre of a Precautionary Area extending up-hbr to the ferry terminal. Caution: Rule 9 (narrow channels) applies. ⚓ in Small Road is not encouraged. Speed limit 5kn N of La Collette Yacht Basin. Approach channels:

- **W Passage** 082° ldg lts and Dog's Nest Rock bcn (unlit W bcn with globe topmark) lead N of Les Fours and Ruaudière Rock SHM lt buoys, to WPT. Beware race off Noirmont Pt.
- **NW Passage** (095°/110°, much used by yachts) passes 6ca S of La Corbière lt ho to join W Passage abm Noirmont Pt.
- **Danger Rock Passage** (044°) unlit; leads past rky, drying shoals; needs precision and good visibility.
- **Red & Green Passage** Ldg line 022·7° passes over Fairway Rk 1·2m, 8ca SSW of the WPT, with drying rks either side; thence via Small Road to the ferry terminal, where daymarks are red dayglow patches on front dolphin and rear lt twr. The fairway's W side is beaconed and buoyed. Outer pier hds and dolphin are painted white and floodlit.
- **S Passage** (341°), unlit marks are hard to see. Demie de Pas in transit 350° with floodlit power stn chy is easier to see D/N.
- **E Passage** 290° from Canger Rock WCM lt buoy passes close SW of Demie de Pas, B tr/Y top (at night stay in W sector); thence 314° past Hinguette buoy and 341° to the WPT.

Other Passages Middle Passage, unlit, leads 339° towards St Aubin Hbr. Violet Channel skirts round SE tip of Jersey to/from the N and would normally link to the E Passage to/from St Helier; see 9.19.5. Caution: many offlying reefs.

LIGHTS AND MARKS See chartlet and 9.19.4 for lights. Power station chy (95m, floodlit), Sig mast, W concave roofs of Fort Regent and Elizabeth Castle are conspic in the harbour area.

IPTS (Sigs 1-4) are shown from the Port Control tower and are easily seen from Small Road and the Main Hbr. An Oc Y 4s, shown above Sigs 1-4, exempts power-driven craft <25m LOA from the main signals. All leisure craft should: *Keep to stbd, well clear of shipping; maintain a sharp all-round lookout and monitor VHF Ch 14 during arr/dep.*
Sig 2 is also shown when vessels depart the Tanker Basin. Departing tankers, which can be hidden at LW, sound a long blast if small craft are approaching.

R/T Monitor *St Helier Port Control* Ch 14 (H24) for ferry/shipping movements. No marina VHF, but call *Port Control* if essential. Do not use Ch M. If unable to pass messages to *Port Control*, these can be relayed via *Jersey Radio* CRS, Ch **82**, 25¹, 16 (H24) or ☎ 741121. ¹available for link calls by charge card.

St Helier Pierheads on Ch 18 broadcasts recorded wind direction, speed and gusts meaned over the last 2 minutes.

TELEPHONE (Code 01534) Port HM 885588, 🖷 885599; ⊖ 833833; Jersey Radio 741121; Marinecall 09068 969656; Police 612612; Dr 835742 and 853178; 🄷 622000.

FACILITIES **Hbrs Dept** ☎ 885588, 🖷 885599. www.jersey-harbours.com jerseyharbours@jersey-harbours.com FW, C (32 ton), Slip, Grids. Basins from seaward:

La Collette basin, good shelter in 1·8m. Access H24; 130 berths only for local boats and FVs, ie no ♥ berths. Caution: Ent narrow at LWS; keep close to W side; PHM buoys mark shoal on E side. ☎ 885529; access H24. BH (65 & 16 ton, ☎ 885573), Slip.

St Helier YC ☎ 721307, R, Bar. **S Pier** (below YC) D & P (access approx HW±3), FW. **Services:** SM, CH, ✕, ME, El, Ⓔ, Gas.
St Helier marina Access HW±3 over sill drying 3·6m; hinged gate rises 1·4m above sill to retain 5m. Digital gauge shows depth when more than 2·2m over sill. IPTS then control ent/exit. A 150m long waiting pontoon is SW of marina ent, with FW & AC; rafting and overnight stays are permitted.

♥ berths: yachts >12m LOA or >2·1m draft, use pontoon A. Smaller craft on fingers N side of D and on E in 2m; or rafted alongside F & G pontoons in 2m; or as directed, £2.04. CH, ME, El, ✕, Grid, Gas, Gaz, 🗑, 🖃.

Extract 7: Cherbourg Tide Table

TIME ZONE -0100	CHERBOURG LAT 49°39'N LONG 1°38'W	Dates in red are SPRINGS
Subtract 1 hour for UT	TIMES AND HEIGHTS OF HIGH AND LOW WATERS	Dates in blue are NEAPS
For French Summer Time add ONE hour in non-shaded areas		YEAR 2007

MAY

Day	Time m	Time m	Time m	Time m		Day	Time m	Time m	Time m	Time m
1 TU	0245 1.6	0818 5.9	1500 1.5	2035 6.0		16 W	0233 1.1	0809 6.4	1453 0.9	2031 6.4
2 W	0317 1.5	0850 5.9	1531 1.5	2105 6.0		17 TH	0322 0.9	0859 6.4	1540 0.9	2117 6.5
3 TH	0348 1.4	0920 5.9	1600 1.5	2133 6.0		18 F	0408 0.9	0946 6.4	1625 1.1	2200 6.4
4 F	0418 1.4	0949 5.9	1630 1.6	2201 6.0		19 SA	0454 1.0	1032 6.2	1709 1.3	2244 6.2
5 SA	0449 1.5	1020 5.8	1700 1.7	2232 5.9		20 SU	0538 1.2	1117 5.9	1754 1.7	2327 6.0
6 SU	0521 1.6	1054 5.6	1732 1.9	2306 5.7		21 M	0624 1.5	1204 5.6	1841 2.0	
7 M	0555 1.8	1131 5.4	1808 2.1	2344 5.5		22 TU	0013 5.6	0713 1.8	1254 5.3	1933 2.4
8 TU	0636 2.0	1215 5.1	1853 2.4			23 W	0105 5.3	0807 2.1	1354 5.0	2034 2.6
9 W	0031 5.2	0728 2.2	1311 4.9	1954 2.6		24 TH	0208 5.0	0910 2.3	1503 4.8	2142 2.7
10 TH	0134 5.0	0836 2.3	1429 4.8	2114 2.7		25 F	0317 4.9	1016 2.4	1610 4.9	2248 2.6
11 F	0257 4.9	0956 2.3	1558 4.9	2236 2.5		26 SA	0423 4.9	1118 2.3	1710 5.0	2348 2.5
12 SA	0419 5.1	1111 2.0	1708 5.2	2346 2.2		27 SU	0523 5.0	1214 2.2	1800 5.2	
13 SU	0526 5.5	1215 1.7	1804 5.6			28 M	0042 2.3	0615 5.2	1302 2.1	1844 5.4
14 M	0049 1.7	0624 5.8	1312 1.3	1855 6.0		29 TU	0128 2.1	0702 5.4	1346 1.9	1924 5.6
15 TU	0143 1.4	0718 6.2	1404 1.1	1944 6.3		30 W	0208 1.9	0744 5.5	1424 1.8	2002 5.8
						31 TH	0246 1.7	0822 5.6	1500 1.8	2037 5.9

JUNE

Day	Time m	Time m	Time m	Time m		Day	Time m	Time m	Time m	Time m
1 F	0322 1.6	0858 5.7	1535 1.7	2110 5.9		16 SA	0356 1.1	0936 6.1	1612 1.4	2148 6.3
2 SA	0358 1.5	0933 5.7	1611 1.7	2145 5.9		17 SU	0443 1.1	1023 6.0	1658 1.5	2233 6.2
3 SU	0435 1.5	1009 5.7	1647 1.8	2221 5.9		18 M	0528 1.2	1108 5.9	1743 1.7	2317 6.0
4 M	0512 1.5	1048 5.7	1725 1.9	2301 5.8		19 TU	0612 1.4	1151 5.7	1826 1.9	
5 TU	0552 1.6	1130 5.5	1806 2.0	2344 5.7		20 W	0000 5.8	0654 1.6	1233 5.5	1910 2.1
6 W	0635 1.7	1216 5.4	1854 2.1			21 TH	0043 5.6	0737 1.9	1317 5.3	1955 2.3
7 TH	0031 5.5	0725 1.8	1304 5.3	1949 2.3		22 F	0127 5.3	0821 2.1	1404 5.1	2045 2.4
8 F	0125 5.4	0821 1.9	1407 5.2	2052 2.3		23 SA	0217 5.1	0911 2.2	1457 4.9	2141 2.6
9 SA	0228 5.3	0925 1.9	1514 5.2	2200 2.3		24 SU	0313 4.9	1008 2.3	1557 4.9	2243 2.6
10 SU	0336 5.3	1032 1.9	1622 5.3	2308 2.1		25 M	0416 4.8	1110 2.5	1659 5.0	2345 2.6
11 M	0445 5.4	1138 1.8	1726 5.5			26 TU	0522 4.9	1211 2.5	1758 5.1	
12 TU	0015 1.9	0551 5.5	1240 1.6	1824 5.8		27 W	0044 2.4	0623 5.0	1306 2.3	1849 5.3
13 W	0116 1.6	0653 5.8	1339 1.5	1920 6.0		28 TH	0135 2.2	0715 5.2	1353 2.2	1934 5.5
14 TH	0213 1.4	0752 6.0	1433 1.4	2012 6.2		29 F	0220 1.9	0801 5.4	1437 2.0	2015 5.7
15 F	0306 1.2	0846 6.1	1524 1.4	2101 6.3		30 SA	0303 1.7	0843 5.6	1518 1.8	2055 5.9

JULY

Day	Time m	Time m	Time m	Time m		Day	Time m	Time m	Time m	Time m
1 SU	0344 1.5	0922 5.7	1537 1.7	2134 6.0		16 M	0433 1.1	1013 6.0	1647 1.5	2222 6.3
2 M	0425 1.4	1002 5.8	1639 1.6	2214 6.1		17 TU	0514 1.1	1052 6.0	1726 1.5	2300 6.2
3 TU	0505 1.3	1042 5.9	1720 1.6	2255 6.1		18 W	0551 1.2	1128 5.9	1803 1.6	2336 6.0
4 W	0546 1.2	1124 5.8	1802 1.6	2338 6.0		19 TH	0626 1.4	1202 5.7	1837 1.8	
5 TH	0628 1.3	1207 5.8	1846 1.7			20 F	0011 5.8	0654 1.6	1236 5.5	1912 2.0
6 F	0021 5.9	0712 1.4	1252 5.6	1933 1.8		21 SA	0043 5.5	0732 1.9	1309 5.3	1949 2.3
7 SA	0107 5.8	0759 1.6	1339 5.5	2025 2.0		22 SU	0119 5.2	0809 2.3	1347 5.1	2033 2.6
8 SU	0158 5.6	0853 1.8	1434 5.4	2126 2.2		23 M	0202 4.9	0855 2.6	1438 4.9	2131 2.8
9 M	0259 5.4	0955 2.0	1540 5.3	2235 2.2		24 TU	0301 4.7	0959 2.8	1548 4.8	2246 2.8
10 TU	0413 5.3	1106 2.1	1654 5.3	2348 2.1		25 W	0425 4.6	1119 2.8	1712 4.8	
11 W	0531 5.3	1218 2.1	1805 5.5			26 TH	0003 2.7	0552 4.7	1232 2.7	1820 5.1
12 TH	0101 1.9	0644 5.5	1325 1.9	1908 5.7		27 F	0108 2.4	0655 5.0	1330 2.4	1913 5.4
13 F	0203 1.6	0748 5.7	1424 1.8	2004 6.0		28 SA	0200 2.0	0745 5.3	1419 2.1	1958 5.7
14 SA	0259 1.4	0843 5.9	1516 1.6	2055 6.1		29 SU	0246 1.7	0829 5.6	1503 1.8	2041 6.0
15 SU	0348 1.2	0931 6.0	1604 1.5	2140 6.2		30 M	0330 1.4	0910 5.9	1546 1.5	2122 6.2
						31 TU	0411 1.1	0950 6.1	1627 1.3	2202 6.4

AUGUST

Day	Time m	Time m	Time m	Time m		Day	Time m	Time m	Time m	Time m
1 W	0452 0.9	1030 6.2	1707 1.2	2243 6.4		16 TH	0522 1.2	1057 6.1	1732 1.4	2305 6.2
2 TH	0531 0.9	1110 6.2	1747 1.2	2323 6.4		17 F	0551 1.3	1126 5.9	1801 1.6	2333 6.0
3 F	0610 0.9	1149 6.1	1828 1.3			18 SA	0618 1.6	1152 5.7	1829 1.9	
4 SA	0004 6.3	0650 1.1	1228 6.0	1910 1.5		19 SU	0000 5.7	0645 1.9	1218 5.5	1859 2.2
5 SU	0044 6.0	0733 1.4	1309 5.7	1957 1.9		20 M	0027 5.3	0715 2.3	1248 5.2	1935 2.5
6 M	0130 5.6	0822 1.9	1357 5.4	2055 2.2		21 TU	0102 5.0	0751 2.6	1328 4.9	2024 2.8
7 TU	0230 5.3	0923 2.3	1505 5.2	2210 2.4		22 W	0155 4.6	0847 3.0	1434 4.6	2141 3.0
8 W	0355 5.0	1045 2.5	1637 5.1	2338 2.4		23 TH	0328 4.4	1024 3.1	1627 4.6	2324 2.9
9 TH	0531 5.0	1212 2.5	1802 5.3			24 F	0530 4.6	1205 2.9	1757 4.9	
10 F	0059 2.1	0650 5.3	1324 2.2	1909 5.6		25 SA	0044 2.5	0637 5.0	1310 2.5	1853 5.3
11 SA	0202 1.8	0750 5.6	1422 1.9	2002 5.9		26 SU	0139 2.0	0726 5.4	1359 2.1	1938 5.7
12 SU	0254 1.4	0838 5.9	1510 1.6	2047 6.2		27 M	0225 1.6	0809 5.8	1444 1.6	2021 6.1
13 M	0338 1.2	0918 6.1	1551 1.4	2127 6.3		28 TU	0308 1.2	0850 6.1	1526 1.3	2102 6.4
14 TU	0416 1.1	0954 6.1	1628 1.4	2202 6.4		29 W	0350 0.9	0930 6.4	1606 1.0	2142 6.7
15 W	0451 1.1	1027 6.1	1701 1.4	2235 6.3		30 TH	0429 0.7	1009 6.5	1646 0.9	2222 6.7
						31 F	0508 0.6	1047 6.5	1725 0.9	2302 6.7

HAT is 7.0 metres above Chart Datum

Extract 8: Cherbourg Tidal Curve

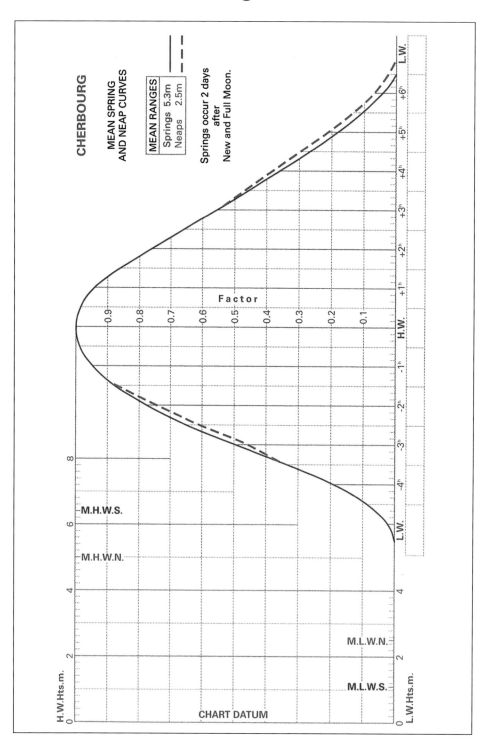

Extract 9: Cherbourg Port Information

CHERBOURG

CHARTS AC *2656, 2669, 1106,* 2602; SHOM 7120, 7092, 7086; Navi 528, 1014; Imray C32, C33A; Stanfords 1, 2, 7, 16, 21.

TIDES Cherbourg is a Standard Port (◄—). –0308 Dover; ML 3·8; Duration 0535; Zone –0100

SHELTER Excellent; a port of refuge available H24 in all tides and weather. Small craft ⌘ N of marina bkwtr in 2·3m, keeping clear of the charted limits of the military port, close N and W.

NAVIGATION For coastal features from Pte de Barfleur to Cap de la Hague see 9.17.5. The Grande Rade is entered via:
- **Passe de l'Ouest** (W ent). WPT 49°41'·05N 01°39'·81W, 141°/ 0·85M to abeam Fort de l'Ouest. Rks, marked by a PHM buoy, Fl R 4s, off Fort de l'Ouest, extend about 80m off each bkwtr. From W, the white sector of Fort de l'Ouest lt (or by day bearing >122°) keeps clear of offlying dangers E of Cap de la Hague. From CH1 SWM buoy, L Fl 10s, Fort de l'Ouest bears 145°/3·5M.
- **Passe de l'Est** (E ent, least depth 8m). WPT 49°40'·91N 01°35'·55W, 189°/0·65M to abeam Fort de l'Est. Keep to W side of chan (but at least 80m off Fort de l'Est) to avoid dangers W and NW of Ile Pelée marked by two PHM lt buoys. N/NE of Ile Pelée an extensive drying area is marked by 2 unlit bn trs.
- **Passe Collignon** is a shallow (2m) chan, 93m wide, through Digue de l'Est (covers), near the shore. Tidal stream reaches 3·4 knots. Only advised in good conditions, near HW.

No anchoring in the Passe de L'Ouest and Passe de L'Est. Speed limits: Grande Rade 14kn, Petite Rade 8kn. No entry to: the area S of the Digue Centrale due to fish farms, nor to the area east of the Port Militaire. Keep clear of ferries.

LIGHTS AND MARKS Daymarks include the chimney of Jobourg nuclear plant, 10M W; the cranes of the naval base; and higher ground S of the city. Five powerful lights assist a good cross-Channel landfall:

- 13M E, Pte de Barfleur, Fl (2) 10s 29M
- 5M ENE, Cap Lévi, Fl R 5s 22M
- 12M WNW, Cap de la Hague, Fl 5s 23M
- 20M W, Alderney, Fl (4) 15s 23M
- 28M W, Casquets, Fl (5) 30s 24M

See also 9.17.4 and 9.19.4.

Passe de l'Ouest ldg lts 141·2° are a Dir Q rear ldg lt aligned between two Q front ldg lts (horizontally disposed) at base of Digue du Homet. Other lts as on chartlet and 9.17.4. On entering the Petite Rade make good 200° for marina ent, Fl (3) R 12s and Fl (3) G 12s. Shore lights may confusingly mask navigational lts.

R/T Marina: *Chantereyne* Ch 09. Commercial port: call *Le Homet* Ch 12 16. Lock (for Bassin du Commerce) Ch 06.

Jobourg Traffic Ch **13** 80 (H24) provides radar surveillance of the Casquets TSS and ITZ and Mont St Michel to Cap d'Antifer. Radar assistance available on request, Ch 80, to vessels in the 270° sector from S clockwise to E, radius 40M from CROSS Jobourg at 49°41'·1N 01°54'·5W. Jobourg broadcasts nav, weather and traffic info in English and French Ch 80 at H+20 & H+50.

TELEPHONE HM (Port) 02·33·20·41·25; Lock 02·33·44·23·18; Aff Mar 02·33·23·36·00; ⊜ 02·33·23·34·02; CROSS 02·33·52·72·13; Météo 02·33·53·53·44; Auto 08.92.68.08.50; Police 02·33·92·70·00; 🏥 02·33·20·70·00; Dr 02·33·53·05·68; Brit Consul 02.33.78.01.83.

FACILITIES Marina ☎ 02·33·87·65·70; ⚓ 02·33·53·21·12. cherbourg.marina@wanadoo.fr Access H24; 985 + 300 Ⓥ on M, N, P, Q pontoons in 2·6m; €2.37. Detached pontoon for larger yachts. Night shwrs via coded S door. P & D 0800-1200, 1400-1900. ME, El, Ⓔ, ✹, CH, SM, SHOM, Slip, BH (30 ton), ⚓, ◙.
Bassin du Commerce is for longer stay; enter via a gate and swing bridge (busy road tfc) which opens HW ±45 mins on request to *Vigie du Homet* Ch 06; 22+18 Ⓥ berths. €9.08/week.
YC de Cherbourg ☎ 02·33·53·02·83, ⚓ 02·33·94·13·73, R, Bar.
City Gaz, ☵, R, Bar, Wi-fi, ✉, ◙, Ⓑ, ⇌. ✈ ☎ 02·33.22.91.32.
Ferry: Portsmouth, Poole.

MINOR HARBOURS EAST OF CHERBOURG

PORT DE LÉVI, Manche, **49°41'·23 N 01°28'·46W**. AC *1106*; SHOM 7120, 5609, 7092; HW –0310 on Dover (UT); +0024 on Cherbourg. HW ht +0·2m on Cherbourg. Shelter good except in SW to N winds. By day appr on 094° keeping the white wall and lt between the white marks on each pier hd. Lt is Oc (2) WRG 6s; see 9.17.4. Keep in W sector (083°-105°), but night entry not advised due to many pot floats. Secure bows on to NE side below white wall, amongst small FVs. Dries to clean sand. Facilities: Peace. Fermanville (1·5M) has ☵, R, Bar.

PORT DU BECQUET, Manche, **49°39'·304N 01°32'·81W**. AC *1106*; SHOM 7120, 7092. Tides as 9.17.30. Ldg lts/marks 186·5°: Both Dir Oc (2+1) 12s (front lt White; rear lt Red), W 8-sided twrs; see 9.17.4. Large PHM bcn twr, La Tounette, marks rks close E. Shelter is good except in winds from N to E when a strong scend enters. Dries to clean sand. Secure to S of the E/W jetty, but there is little space. Facilities: very few; all facilities at Cherbourg 2·5M.

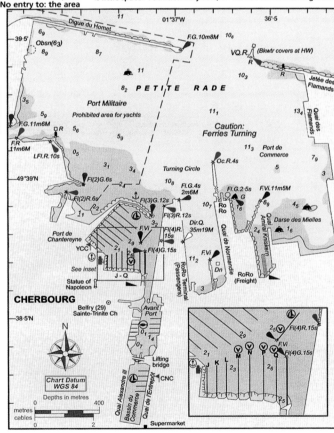

Extract 10: Cherbourg Chart

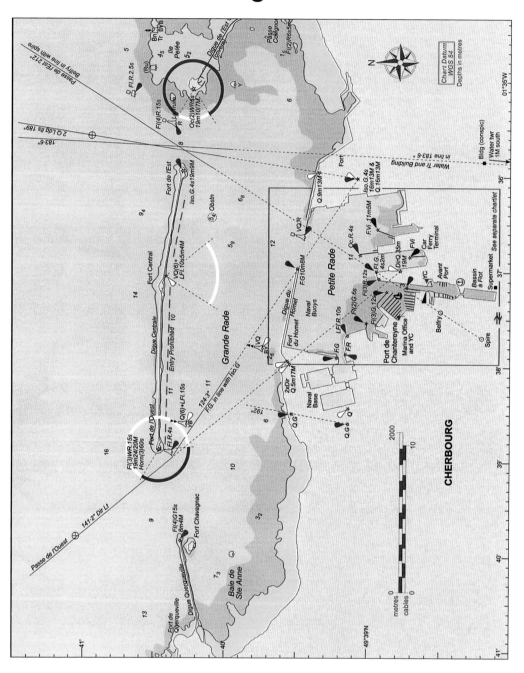

Extract 11: Approaches to St Peter Port

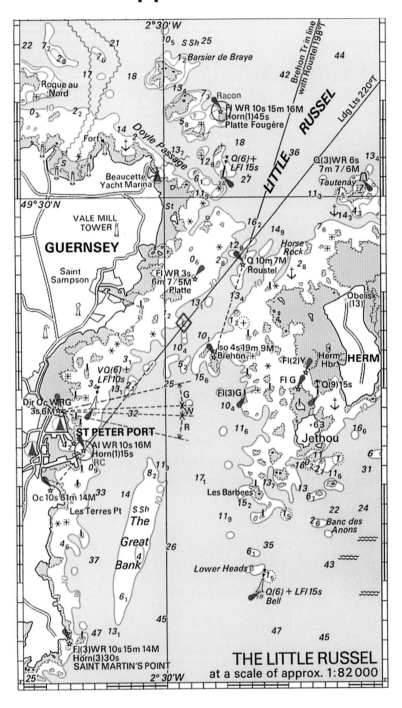

Extract 12: St Peter Port Information

ST PETER PORT

TIDES −0439 Dover; ML 5·2; Duration 0550; Zone 0 (UT)

NOTE: St Peter Port is a Standard Port, see Tide Tables overleaf.

To find depth of water over the sill into Victoria marina:
1. Look up predicted time and height of HW St Peter Port.
2. Enter table below on the line for height of HW.
3. Extract depth (m) of water for time before/after HW.

Ht (m) of HW St Peter Port	Depth of Water in metres over the Sill (dries 4·2 m)						
	HW	±1hr	±2hrs	±2½hrs	±3hrs	±3½hrs	±4hrs
6·20	2·00	1·85	1·55	1·33	1·10	0·88	0·65
·60	2·40	2·18	1·75	1·43	1·10	0·77	0·45
7·00	2·80	2·52	1·95	1·53	1·10	0·67	0·25
·40	3·20	2·85	2·15	1·63	1·10	0·57	0·05
·80	3·60	3·18	2·35	1·73	1·10	0·47	0·00
8·20	4·00	3·52	2·55	1·83	1·10	0·37	0·00
·60	4·40	3·85	2·75	1·93	1·10	0·28	0·00
9·00	4·80	4·18	2·95	2·03	1·10	0·18	0·00
·40	5·20	4·52	3·15	2·13	1·10	0·08	0·00
·80	5·60	4·85	3·35	2·23	1·10	0·00	0·00

SHELTER Good, especially in Victoria Marina which has a sill 4·2m above CD, with a gauge giving depth over sill. Access approx HW±2½ according to draft; see Table above. R/G tfc lts control ent/exit. Appr via buoyed/lit chan via S side of hbr. Marina boat will direct yachts to waiting pontoon or Ⓥ pontoons with FW (nos 1-5) N of the waiting pontoon. Pontoons for tenders are each side of marina ent. ♣ prohib. Ⓥ berths in centre of hbr, with a secondary fairway N of them. ♣ prohib. Ⓥ berths in Queen Elizabeth II and Albert marinas by prior arrangement.

NAVIGATION WPT 49°27'·82N 02°30'·78W, 227°/0·68M to hbr ent. Offlying dangers, big tidal range and strong tidal streams demand careful navigation. Easiest appr from N is via Big Russel between Herm and Sark, passing S of Lower Hds SCM lt buoy. The Little Russel is slightly more direct, but needs care especially in poor visibility; see 9.19.5 and 9.19.9 chartlet. From W and S of Guernsey, give Les Hanois a wide berth. Beware ferries and shipping. Hbr speed limits: 6kn from outer pier heads to line from New Jetty to Castle Cornet; 4kn W of that line.

An **RDF beacon, GY** 304·50kHz, on Castle Bkwtr is synchronised with the co-located horn* to give distance finding. The horn blast begins simultaneously with the 27 sec long dash following the four GY ident signals. Time the number of seconds from the start of the long dash until the horn blast is heard, multiply by 0·18 = your distance in M from the horn; several counts are advised.

LIGHTS AND MARKS Outer ldg lts 220°: Front, Castle bkwtr hd Al WR 10s (vis 187°-007°) Horn 15s*; rear, Belvedere Oc 10s 61m 14M, intens 217°-223°. By day, White patch at Castle Cornet in line 223° with Belvedere Ho (conspic). Inner ldg lts 265°: Front, Oc R 5s; rear, Iso R 2s, vis 260°-270° (10°). This ldg line is for the use of ferries berthing at New Jetty. It extends through moorings in The Pool, so must not be used by yachts which should appr Victoria marina via the buoyed/lit S channel (dashed line).
Traffic Signals on White Rock (N) pierhead:
● (vis from seaward) = No entry.
● (vis from landward) = No exit (and at New Pier, SW corner). These sigs do not apply to boats, <15m LOA, under power and keeping clear of the fairways.

R/T St Peter Port Marina Ch M 80 (office hrs). Monitor St Peter Port Control VHF Ch **12** (H24) but call Port Control if necessary when within the pilotage area. Water taxi Ch 10 (0800-2359LT). Call St Peter Port Radio CRS Ch 20 for safety traffic. Link calls Ch 62. St Sampson Ch 12 (H24).

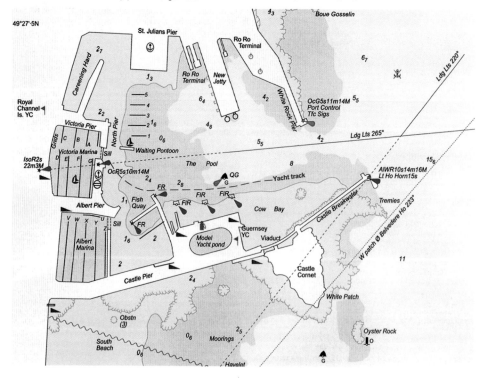

Extract 13: St Malo Tide Tables

TIME ZONE -0100	ST MALO LAT 48°38′N · LONG 2°02′W	
Subtract 1 hour for UT For French Summer Time add ONE hour in non-shaded areas	TIMES AND HEIGHTS OF HIGH AND LOW WATERS	Dates in red are SPRINGS Dates in blue are NEAPS YEAR 2007

MAY

Day	Time m	Day	Time m
1 TU	0101 2.6 / 0631 11.1 / 1320 2.4 / 1850 11.3	16 W	0059 1.7 / 0628 12.1 / 1324 1.4 / ● 1849 12.2
2 W	0135 2.3 / 0704 11.3 / 1352 2.3 / ○ 1921 11.5	17 TH	0150 1.4 / 0716 12.3 / 1412 1.3 / 1934 12.4
3 TH	0207 2.2 / 0735 11.4 / 1422 2.2 / 1951 11.6	18 F	0237 1.3 / 0801 12.3 / 1455 1.4 / 2017 12.4
4 F	0238 2.2 / 0805 11.4 / 1450 2.3 / 2019 11.5	19 SA	0320 1.4 / 0845 12.0 / 1536 1.8 / 2058 12.0
5 SA	0308 2.3 / 0834 11.2 / 1519 2.5 / 2046 11.3	20 SU	0401 1.9 / 0928 11.4 / 1615 2.4 / 2140 11.5
6 SU	0338 2.5 / 0904 11.0 / 1548 2.9 / 2116 11.0	21 M	0440 2.5 / 1012 10.8 / 1654 3.1 / 2224 10.8
7 M	0410 2.9 / 0937 10.5 / 1620 3.4 / 2151 10.5	22 TU	0522 3.2 / 1059 10.0 / 1738 3.8 / 2313 10.1
8 TU	0446 3.4 / 1017 10.0 / 1658 3.9 / 2233 9.9	23 W	0608 3.8 / 1153 9.4 / 1830 4.4 / ◑
9 W	0530 3.8 / 1108 9.4 / 1748 4.4 / 2334 9.4	24 TH	0013 9.5 / 0706 4.3 / 1300 9.0 / 1936 4.7
10 TH	0631 4.2 / 1221 9.0 / 1901 4.7 / ◔	25 F	0124 9.1 / 0814 4.5 / 1414 9.0 / 2047 4.6
11 F	0102 9.2 / 0752 4.2 / 1352 9.0 / 2033 4.5	26 SA	0236 9.2 / 0922 4.3 / 1520 9.2 / 2151 4.3
12 SA	0230 9.5 / 0919 3.8 / 1511 9.6 / 2154 3.8	27 SU	0337 9.4 / 1021 4.0 / 1613 9.7 / 2245 3.9
13 SU	0342 10.2 / 1031 3.1 / 1616 10.3 / 2300 3.0	28 M	0428 9.8 / 1112 3.6 / 1658 10.1 / 2333 3.5
14 M	0442 10.9 / 1134 2.3 / 1712 11.1	29 TU	0513 10.2 / 1157 3.3 / 1738 10.5
15 TU	0001 2.2 / 0537 11.6 / 1231 1.7 / 1802 11.8	30 W	0018 3.1 / 0554 10.5 / 1239 3.0 / 1815 10.9
		31 TH	0058 2.8 / 0632 10.8 / 1317 2.8 / 1851 11.1

JUNE

Day	Time m	Day	Time m
1 F	0136 2.6 / 0709 11.0 / 1353 2.7 / ○ 1925 11.3	16 SA	0219 1.8 / 0750 11.6 / 1437 2.0 / 2004 11.9
2 SA	0213 2.5 / 0744 11.1 / 1428 2.6 / 1959 11.4	17 SU	0305 1.8 / 0836 11.5 / 1521 2.1 / 2048 11.8
3 SU	0250 2.4 / 0819 11.1 / 1503 2.7 / 2033 11.3	18 M	0349 2.0 / 0920 11.3 / 1603 2.4 / 2131 11.5
4 M	0328 2.5 / 0856 11.0 / 1541 2.9 / 2111 11.2	19 TU	0430 2.3 / 1002 10.9 / 1643 2.8 / 2212 11.1
5 TU	0407 2.7 / 0937 10.7 / 1620 3.1 / 2152 10.9	20 W	0509 2.8 / 1043 10.5 / 1723 3.3 / 2254 10.6
6 W	0449 2.9 / 1022 10.4 / 1704 3.4 / 2240 10.5	21 TH	0548 3.3 / 1124 10.0 / 1803 3.7 / 2337 10.0
7 TH	0536 3.2 / 1112 10.1 / 1754 3.7 / 2335 10.1	22 F	0628 3.7 / 1208 9.6 / 1847 4.1 / ◑
8 F	0630 3.5 / 1210 9.8 / 1854 3.9 / ◔	23 SA	0025 9.5 / 0714 4.1 / 1300 9.2 / 1940 4.4
9 SA	0040 9.9 / 0733 3.6 / 1317 9.7 / 2003 3.9	24 SU	0121 9.2 / 0808 4.3 / 1402 9.1 / 2040 4.5
10 SU	0151 10.0 / 0842 3.5 / 1428 9.8 / 2115 3.7	25 M	0226 9.1 / 0911 4.4 / 1508 9.2 / 2144 4.4
11 M	0301 10.2 / 0952 3.2 / 1536 10.2 / 2224 3.2	26 TU	0331 9.2 / 1015 4.2 / 1609 9.5 / 2244 4.1
12 TU	0408 10.6 / 1059 2.8 / 1639 10.7 / 2329 2.7	27 W	0429 9.5 / 1113 3.9 / 1700 9.9 / 2338 3.7
13 W	0509 11.0 / 1200 2.4 / 1736 11.2	28 TH	0520 9.9 / 1204 3.6 / 1746 10.4
14 TH	0032 2.3 / 0611 11.3 / 1257 2.1 / 1829 11.6	29 F	0028 3.2 / 0607 10.3 / 1250 3.2 / 1829 10.8
15 F	0128 2.0 / 0700 11.6 / 1349 2.0 / ● 1918 11.9	30 SA	0113 2.9 / 0651 10.7 / 1333 2.9 / ○ 1909 11.1

JULY

Day	Time m	Day	Time m
1 SU	0157 2.6 / 0732 10.9 / 1416 2.7 / 1949 11.4	16 M	0256 1.9 / 0827 11.5 / 1511 2.1 / 2038 11.9
2 M	0241 2.3 / 0813 11.2 / 1458 2.5 / 2028 11.6	17 TU	0338 1.9 / 0906 11.5 / 1551 2.1 / 2116 11.8
3 TU	0325 2.1 / 0853 11.3 / 1540 2.4 / 2109 11.6	18 W	0415 2.0 / 0942 11.3 / 1627 2.3 / 2151 11.5
4 W	0408 2.1 / 0935 11.3 / 1623 2.4 / 2151 11.5	19 TH	0449 2.3 / 1016 11.0 / 1659 2.7 / 2225 11.1
5 TH	0451 2.2 / 1018 11.1 / 1706 2.6 / 2235 11.3	20 F	0518 2.8 / 1048 10.5 / 1729 3.2 / 2257 10.5
6 F	0534 2.4 / 1102 10.8 / 1750 2.9 / 2321 10.9	21 SA	0546 3.3 / 1120 10.1 / 1800 3.7 / 2331 9.9
7 SA	0619 2.8 / 1149 10.5 / 1838 3.3 / ◔	22 SU	0617 3.8 / 1156 9.5 / 1837 4.2 / ◑
8 SU	0013 10.5 / 0708 3.1 / 1243 10.1 / 1934 3.6	23 M	0012 9.3 / 0657 4.3 / 1243 9.1 / 1927 4.7
9 M	0114 10.1 / 0807 3.4 / 1347 9.9 / 2041 3.8	24 TU	0110 8.8 / 0753 4.7 / 1355 8.7 / 2038 4.9
10 TU	0226 9.9 / 0917 3.6 / 1502 9.9 / 2155 3.7	25 W	0231 8.6 / 0913 4.9 / 1520 8.8 / 2159 4.7
11 W	0340 10.0 / 1030 3.5 / 1617 10.2 / 2308 3.3	26 TH	0351 8.9 / 1034 4.6 / 1631 9.3 / 2308 4.1
12 TH	0456 10.3 / 1140 3.1 / 1724 10.7	27 F	0456 9.4 / 1138 4.1 / 1726 9.9
13 F	0017 2.8 / 0601 10.7 / 1242 2.8 / 1822 11.2	28 SA	0005 3.5 / 0550 10.0 / 1232 3.5 / 1813 10.6
14 SA	0117 2.4 / 0656 11.1 / 1338 2.4 / ● 1912 11.6	29 SU	0058 2.9 / 0638 10.6 / 1321 2.9 / 1857 11.2
15 SU	0210 2.0 / 0744 11.4 / 1427 2.2 / 1956 11.8	30 M	0147 2.3 / 0722 11.1 / 1408 2.4 / ○ 1939 11.7
		31 TU	0235 1.8 / 0803 11.6 / 1453 2.0 / 2019 12.1

AUGUST

Day	Time m	Day	Time m
1 W	0320 1.5 / 0844 11.9 / 1536 1.7 / 2100 12.3	16 TH	0351 1.8 / 0914 11.7 / 1601 2.0 / 2123 11.8
2 TH	0402 1.4 / 0924 12.0 / 1617 1.6 / 2139 12.3	17 F	0418 2.0 / 0943 11.4 / 1627 2.3 / 2151 11.4
3 F	0442 1.4 / 1003 11.8 / 1656 1.8 / 2219 12.0	18 SA	0441 2.5 / 1009 11.0 / 1651 2.8 / 2217 10.8
4 SA	0520 1.8 / 1042 11.5 / 1735 2.3 / 2300 11.5	19 SU	0502 3.0 / 1034 10.4 / 1714 3.4 / 2242 10.2
5 SU	0558 2.4 / 1123 10.9 / 1816 2.9 / ◑ 2344 10.8	20 M	0526 3.6 / 1100 9.8 / 1743 4.1 / 2312 9.5
6 M	0640 3.1 / 1210 10.3 / 1905 3.6	21 TU	0556 4.3 / 1133 9.2 / 1823 4.7 / ◑ 2354 8.8
7 TU	0042 10.0 / 0734 3.8 / 1312 9.7 / 2012 4.1	22 W	0641 4.9 / 1231 8.5 / 1926 5.2
8 W	0200 9.4 / 0848 4.2 / 1440 9.4 / 2138 4.2	23 TH	0124 8.2 / 0758 5.4 / 1342 8.3 / 2112 5.2
9 TH	0337 9.3 / 1016 4.2 / 1613 9.7 / 2302 3.7	24 F	0321 8.4 / 1000 5.2 / 1606 8.9 / 2244 4.6
10 F	0459 9.8 / 1135 3.7 / 1724 10.4	25 SA	0437 9.1 / 1118 4.4 / 1706 9.7 / 2346 3.7
11 SA	0015 3.1 / 0600 10.5 / 1239 3.0 / 1817 11.1	26 SU	0532 10.0 / 1214 3.5 / 1754 10.7
12 SU	0112 2.5 / 0649 11.1 / 1332 2.4 / 1903 11.6	27 M	0042 2.7 / 0620 10.8 / 1305 2.6 / 1839 11.5
13 M	0201 2.0 / 0732 11.5 / 1416 2.0 / ● 1943 11.9	28 TU	0132 2.0 / 0703 11.5 / 1353 1.9 / ○ 1921 12.2
14 TU	0243 1.8 / 0809 11.7 / 1456 1.8 / 2019 12.1	29 W	0220 1.4 / 0745 12.1 / 1438 1.4 / 2002 12.7
15 W	0319 1.7 / 0843 11.8 / 1530 1.8 / 2052 12.0	30 TH	0304 1.0 / 0824 12.5 / 1521 1.1 / 2041 12.9
		31 F	0345 0.8 / 0903 12.6 / 1601 1.1 / 2120 12.8

HAT is 13·6 metres above Chart Datum

Extract 14: St Malo Tidal Curve

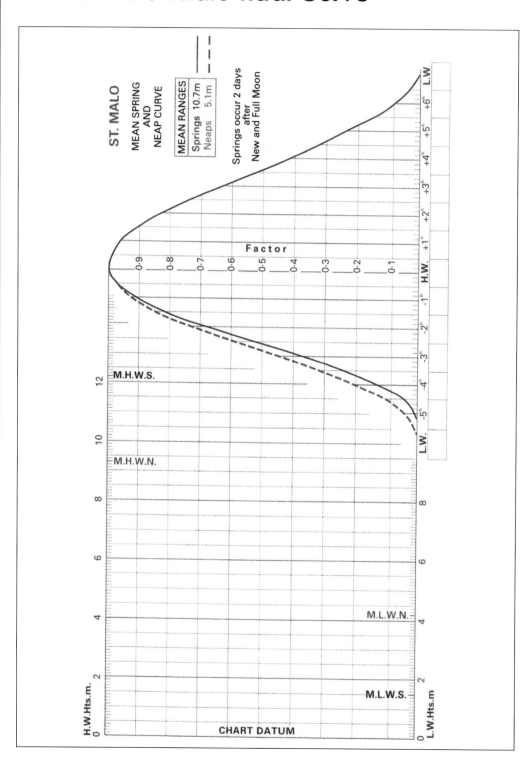

Extract 15: St Malo Approaches

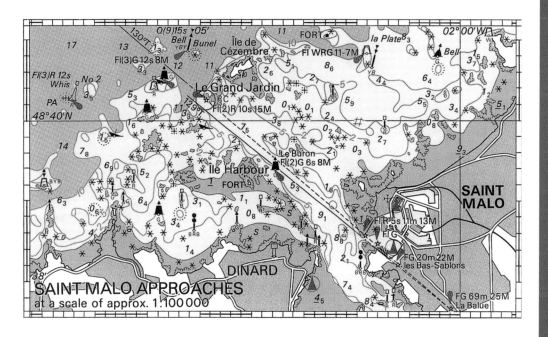

Extract 16: St Malo Port Information

ST MALO

LIGHTS AND MARKS See chartlets/9.18.4 for ldg lts/buoys. Conspic daymarks: Île de Cézembre, Le Grand Jardin lt ho, Le Buron SHM twr, Petit and Grand Bé islets, the W lt twr/R top on Mole des Noires head and St Malo cathedral spire.

R/T Marinas Ch 09. *St Malo Port* Ch **12**.

TELEPHONE Port HM 02·99·20·63·01, ▦ 02·99·56·48·71; Aff Mar 02·99·56·87·00; ⊜ 02·99·81·65·90; CROSS 02·98·89·31·31; Météo 02·99·46·10·46; Auto 08.92.68.08.35; Police 02·99·81·52·30; Ⓗ 02·99·56·56·19; Brit Consul 02.23.18.30.30.

FACILITIES Les Bas-Sablons marina is entered over sill 2m. Access for 1·5m draft approx HW −3½ to +4½ sp; H24 at nps. Two W waiting buoys outside. Depth over sill is shown on a digital gauge atop the S bkwtr, visible only from seaward. Inside, a conventional gauge at base of N bkwtr shows depths <3m.
☎ 02·99·81·71·34, ▦ 02.99.81.91.81. www.ville-saint-malo.fr 1216 + 64 Ⓥ, €2.68. Ⓥ berths on A pontoon: 32-66 (E side) and 43-75 (W side), and on B pontoon: 92-102 and 91-101. Slip, C (2·5 ton), BH (20 ton), Gaz, El, Ⓔ, ME, CH, ⚒, ⛵, SM, SHOM, R, YC, Bar, P & D pontoon 'I'; use French credit card or pay at office.
St Malo/St Servan: Gaz, ▦, R, Bar, ✉, Ⓑ, ⇌. Ferry: Portsmouth, Poole, Weymouth.

Bassin Vauban (6m) is entered by lock. Help is given with warps. Outside the lock are 3 waiting buoys N of appr chan; keep clear of vedette and ferry berths.
Lock times may vary with traffic & tides. Lock is scheduled to operate 5 or 6 times in each direction, relative to HW, ie:

Inward	−2½	−1½	−½	+½	+1½	+2½
Outward	−2		−1	HW	+1	+2

Lock sigs are IPTS Nos 2, 3 and 5. In addition:
next to the top lt = both lock gates are open, ie freeflow, beware current initially. Main message is the same. Freeflow is rare due to busy road traffic over retracting roller bridges.
● ● over ● = all movements prohib, big ship is outbound.
Port Vauban ☎ 02·99·56·51·91, ▦ 02.99.56.57.81 www.saint-

malo.cci.fr portplaisancevauban@saint-malo.cci.fr. 175 + 50 Ⓥ, €3.07. Berth on pontoon marked for your LOA (see inset above); no fingers; no turning room between pontoons 1-3. No ⚓ in basins; 3kn speed limit. C (1 ton). YC ☎ 02·99·40·84·42, Bar (Ⓥ welcome). Bassin Duguay-Trouin is better for long stay.

DINARD Access by 1m marked chan to yacht basin 2m; see inset overleaf (many local boats; best to pre-book). **HM** ☎ 02·99·46·65·55. ⚓, M €1.91 (afloat), €1.25 (drying). Slip, P&D, ME, El, Ⓔ, ⚒, SM. YC ☎ 02·99·46·14·32, R, Bar. **Town** CH, ▦, Gaz, R, Bar, ✉, Ⓑ, ⇌, ✈. Ⓗ 02·99·46·18·68. Ferries to St Malo.

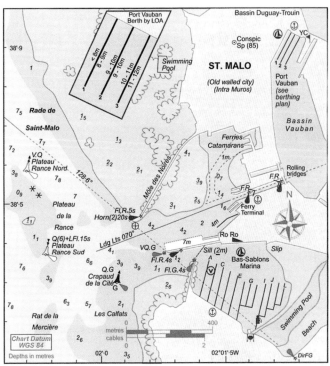

Extract 17: Granville Port Information

GRANVILLE Manche **48°49'·94N 01°35'·93W** (Marina ent) ✦✦✦✦✦✦✦✦

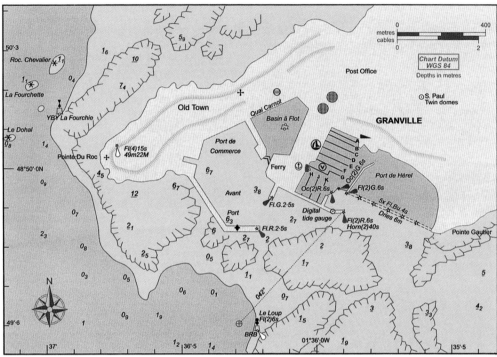

CHARTS AC 3656, *3659*, 3672; SHOM 7156, 7341; Navi 534, 535; Imray C33B; Stanfords 1, 2, 16, 26

TIDES −0510 Dover; ML 7·1; Duration 0525; Zone −0100

Standard Port ST-MALO (→)

Times				Height (metres)			
High Water		Low Water		MHWS	MHWN	MLWN	MLWS
0100	0800	0300	0800	12·2	9·3	4·2	1·5
1300	2000	1500	2000				
Differences REGNÉVILLE-SUR-MER							
+0005	+0005	+0025	+0025	−0·2	−0·2	+0·1	+0·1
GRANVILLE							
+0005	+0005	+0020	+0010	+0·7	+0·5	+0·3	+0·1
CANCALE							
0000	0000	+0010	+0010	+0·8	+0·6	+0·3	+0·1

SHELTER Good in the marina. Appr is rough in strong W winds. ⚓ in 2m about 4ca WSW of Le Loup to await the tide.

NAVIGATION WPT 48°49'·60N 01°36'·30W (abm Le Loup IDM), 042°/0·40M to S bkwtr lt. Beware rks seaward of La Fourchie WCM bcn twr, and port markers off Pte du Roc and 0·4m patches on Banc de Tombelaine, 1M SSW of Le Loup lt. At night best to keep at least 8ca W of Pte du Roc to avoid the worst of these dangers.

At bkwtr hd turn port wide into marina ent to avoid yachts leaving; cross the sill between R/G piles, Fl Bu 4s, mark the covering wall of a windsurfing/dinghy area to stbd. Ent/exit under power; speed limit 5kn in the near approach.

LIGHTS AND MARKS Pte du Roc is a conspic headland with large old bldgs and lt ho, grey twr, R top; the Sig stn and church spire are also obvious. The twin domes of St Paul's church in transit 034° with Le Loup lead towards the marina ent. No ldg lts, but S bkwtr hd on with TV mast leads 057° to ent; hbr lts are hard to see against town lts. 3·5M W of Pte du Roc, Le Videcoq rock drying 0·8m, is marked by a WCM lt buoy. See chartlet and 9.18.4 for lt details.

R/T Port Ch 12, 16 (HW±1½). Marina Ch 09, H24 in season.

TELEPHONE Port HM 02·33·50·17·75; Aff Mar 02·33·91·31·40; CROSS 02·33·52·72·13; SNSM 02·33·61·26·51; ⊖ 02·33·50·19·90; Météo 02·33·22·91·77; Auto 08.92.68.08.50; Police 02·33·50·01·00; Dr 02·33·50·00·07; ⊞ 02·33·90·74·75; Brit Consul 02.23.18.30.30.

FACILITIES Hérel marina Access over sill HW −2½ to +3½. Depth over sill shown on digital display atop S bkwtr: eg 76 = 7·6m; 00 = no entry; hard to read in bright sun. Speed limit 2kn.

☎ 02·33·50·20·06, 🖷 02·33·50·17·01. www.granville.cci.fr pjs@granville.cci.fr 850+150 Ⓥ on pontoon G, 1·5–2·5m. €0.66/m² <20m², €0.49/m² >20m². Slip, P, D, ME, BH (12 ton), C (1·5 ton), CH, Gaz, 🅟, 🗑, SM, El, ✕, 🏧, Ⓔ, SHOM.

YC de Granville ☎ 02·33·50·04·25, 🖷 02·33·50·06·59, Bar, R.

Town P, D, ME, 🗑, Gaz, R, Bar, ⊠, Ⓑ, ⇌, ✈ (Dinard). Ferry: UK via Jersey or Cherbourg.

MINOR HARBOUR 10M NORTH OF GRANVILLE

REGNÉVILLE, Manche, **48°59'·72N 01°34'·05W** (SHM buoy abm Pte d'Agon). AC *3656*; SHOM 7156, 7133. HW −0500 on Dover (UT); ML 7·0m; Duration 0535. See 9.18.10. A seriously drying hbr on the estuary of R. La Sienne; little frequented by yachts, a magnet for hardy adventurers seeking sand and solitude.

From 48°57'·65N 01°38'·86W (2·2M E of La Catheue SCM buoy) identify Pte d'Agon lt ho, W twr/R top, and Regnéville's 028° dir lt, both 4M NE at the river mouth (see 9.18.4). Thence track 056°/3·8M across the drying estuary to the SHM buoy (Lat/Long in line 1) marking a drying mole extending SW from the sandspit to stbd. Here there are landing stages; a small pontoon at Regnéville is 1·2M NNE. Drying heights are around 9m and 12·7m off Pte d'Agon.

Access HW −1 to +2 for 1·3m draft. Approx 80 moorings inc ⚓s. YC ☎ 02·33·46·36·76. **Facilities:** Quay, CH, BY, C (25 ton). **Town:** D&P (cans), Ⓑ, ⊠, Bar, R, 🗑. Tourism ☎ 02·33·45·88·71.